"*Life Happens* caused me to stop and exa[...]
met up with someone who so succinctly [...]
concerns and helps me see where I sorely [...]
toring or modeling, people don't have a cl[...]
differently. I probably own and have read [...] books as I've considered how others interpret the world. Perhaps I had to live this much of life
to recognize how valuable your information is. Your book provides tools
that can be keenly and deftly employed to keep my family strong. Thank
you, thank you."

—Janet Favero Chambers
President and Founder: National Fibromyalgia
& Chronic Pain Association

"Life happens, doesn't it? And struggle enters into every life, sometimes
nearly overwhelming in its magnitude and intensity. In this insightful and
thought-provoking book, Teresa and Taralyn Clark provide us with powerful tools to face personal and family adversity with courage, humor, and
grace through *story*. If you are a member of a family—or a member of the
human family—this book is for you: a roadmap to lead you safely (if not
unscathed) through the hazards of life."

—Sherry Norfolk
Former Chair: National Storytelling Network,
Storyteller, Author, award-winning Teaching Artist

"When faced with adversity and hardship, the first feelings are often that of
loneliness and despair. In their book, *Life Happens: How to Maintain Family Strength and Unity in the Face of Adversity*, Teresa and Taralyn share
many heartwarming experiences of their own family and those of others
that reinforce the powerful message of hope. I highly recommend this
book because it teaches families, who have or who will face difficult circumstances, that humor, love, touch, and time spent together will triumph
over feelings of discouragement and isolation. The result is that families
can be fortified through adversity instead of being pulled apart."

—Jared R. Knight
Manager of Programs: Aspen Grove Family Camp,
Brigham Young University,
Author: *101 Games and Activities to Strengthen Families*

"*Life Happens* . . . is one of those rare books giving us glimpses into the stories of several families persisting and thriving through life's challenges. The book is filled with sweet moments, love, and laughter. It speaks to the heart, soul, and spirit of family as they deal with heartbreaks and find their way through them all. Drawing on faith, courage, love, blessings, and purposeful story sharing they keep going, finding wisdom and inspiration along the way. It is a testament to family and spirit. Everyone will find gems in this book."

—Karen Dietz , Owner:
Just Story It
Former Executive Director, National Storytelling Network

"*Life Happens: How to Maintain Family Strength and Unity in the Face of Adversity* takes the reader on an inspiring journey with families who are dealing with the challenge of chronic illness. Rather than being discouraged by their stories, the reader becomes wrapped in the complex web of sorrow, joy, despair, hope, fear, courage, and the many other emotions we as human beings feel when faced with the unexpected obstacles of life. Taralyn's family research experience and Teresa's gift of storytelling is a happy combination for communicating an important message that can benefit every reader. *Life Happens* . . . is a rewarding experience for any reader who loves family and rejoices in hearing a great story. The family storytelling activity suggestions are invaluable for any family."

—Dr. Kari S. Archibald , Department of Health, Recreation, and
Human Performance, Brigham Young University Idaho

"*Life Happens* . . . is written in story form, which allows the reader to make their own connections, draw their own conclusions, and take away their own lessons. Taralyn and Teresa's ability to capture their own family history may inspire others to look more closely at and share the stories of their own families and, thus, strengthen those they love. The thread of family strength is evident throughout, and while clearly there were many challenges for so many family members, the common positive link that provided strength was their link to family."

—Dr. Julie M. Hite , Educational Leadership & Foundations,
Brigham Young University

"Your book was so readable with excellent examples on how families with strength and unity can survive in the face of adversity. Having it in story form made it so easy to follow each family's story. There was so much to touch the heart, lighten your spirit, and bring solace to your soul. I would give it two thumbs up!

—Jana Firth, Volunteer: Utah Fibromyalgia Association,
Mother, Grandmother, Sister, and chronic illness Warrior

# Life Happens

## HOW TO

## MAINTAIN

## FAMILY STRENGTH

## AND UNITY

## IN THE FACE

## OF ADVERSITY

Taralyn and Teresa Clark

Published by Familius LLC, www.familius.com

Familius books are available at special discounts for bulk
purchases for sales promotions, family or corporate use.
Special editions, including personalized covers, excerpts of
existing books, or books with corporate logos, can be created in
large quantities for special needs. For more information,
contact Premium Sales at 559-876-2170 or email
specialmarkets@familius.com

Library of Congress Catalog-in-Publication Data
LCCN 2013941691
pISBN 978-1-938301-78-0
eISBN 978-1-939629-92-0

Printed in the United States of America

Edited by Emily Smith
Book design by Kurt Wahlner

First Edition

# Table of Contents

# Dedication

*We dedicate this work to
Stuart Lynn Clark, without whom
there is no story. Glory be to God
for any good that comes from these
pages, we pray they may touch your
heart and bless your life!*

# Acknowlegements

We are aware a project such as this cannot be accomplished alone. We owe a great debt of gratitude to all who have helped us along our journey.

Glory goes to God first and foremost, the great Teacher and Exemplar. He has entrusted us with experiences that enable us to reach others. Our hope and prayer is that He can reach you through this work.

Thanks go next to our family and friends who have shared their stories with us. Unless express permission was given to use real names, all names in this work have been changed to protect those who have entrusted us with their stories. Special thanks go to the families who opened their hearts and homes to Taralyn as she conducted her thesis research, and also to her faculty advisor and friend, Stacy Taniguchi PhD, who made her research possible.

Our family, roommates, employers, and friends have been impacted by the amount of time spent on this project. We'd like to thank them for their love, patience, and willingness to allow us time and space to fulfill the dream of sharing these stories with you.

We would like to express appreciation to Christopher Robbins and Familius Publishing for believing in this project from the beginning. We would also like to thank the editors and proofreaders who helped to polish our work into something worth publishing.

# Introduction

Ironically, we both felt sucker punched just as Familius sent us the contract to share these stories with you. We hadn't come down with any life-threatening illnesses, but by the way we reacted to the insidious bugs waging war on our productivity and well-being, you would think we had. Admittedly, we had nothing more than colds. Yet, this book sat untouched for weeks as we both recovered because neither one of us could muster the fortitude to tackle the process in our weakened states.

As we lay in our sickbeds of affliction, slipping in and out of cold medicine-induced dreams of dancing hippos and spinning sea turtles, we independently expressed feeling ashamed of the effect a simple cold was having on us and therefore everyone around us. Then we began talking about this book and Stuart, the patriarch of our family. He has been battling chronic respiratory illness for nearly ten years, and he doubles as our hero. While a little cold has the power to knock us both flat on our backs, he has felt at least that uncomfortable every day since the onset of his illness. The weariness, sinus pressure, body aches, tickly throat, coughing, sneezing, labored breathing, and medicinal effects have been his constant companions. While we knew our colds would pass, he knows he'll never feel completely normal again. Add unforeseen side effects, complications, surgeries, and never-ending doctor visits to the ongoing symptoms, and it becomes easy to see why we hold this man in such high regard. Stuart continues to work to support our family, spend time with each of us, serve in our church and community, and bless the lives of others. We have never once heard him ask, "Why me?" He simply accepts his fate and moves on. This may sound a little warped, but what an incredible blessing his chronic illness has been for our family! We hope you'll understand by the end of this book why we count his crucible of affliction as one of our family's choicest blessings.

We know something about living with a husband and father battling chronic illness. We also know a great number of people who deal with the same problems and worse, but what really qualifies us to write this book anyway? Good question. We do not in any way believe we know more than you. We are well aware that every man, woman, and child has something to teach us. We know this because we are lovers of story! We believe stories are living, breathing things with power to instruct, uplift, enlighten, and bless. We know your story has power to teach us just as ours has power to teach you.

Because we know the power of story, we have spent decades collecting the stories of people just like us: People who face insurmountable odds yet somehow find a way to wake up every morning, keep a smile on their faces, and remain close as families in spite of situations that make such closeness increasingly difficult. Taralyn's thesis research with families facing adult-onset chronic illness was a direct result of her experiences at home, and it substantiated six well-known characteristics of strong families (appreciation, effective communication, time together, spirituality, coping well with crisis, and commitment). Her research also unearthed the important role of maintaining family unity via four key actions (telling family stories, establishing and maintaining a unified perspective, setting common goals, and practicing an attitude of service) when faced with trying circumstances in family life.

Similarly, Teresa's story work has revealed seven key identity stories every family should know and share (creation, origin, sacred, shorthand, gratitude, success, and divine diversions). Read on to see how families intentionally and unintentionally use these tools to strengthen and lift each other. These stories may not be your stories, but we believe you will find the emotions and concerns they explore hit home. It is our hope these stories will empower you to purposefully spend time shoring up your own family identity to protect against your next sucker punch.

If your family is anything like ours, you are a bit wary of books like this. After all, who can really understand what you're going through? If we're being honest, we have to admit we don't know exactly what you're going through.

However, we do know the principles are the same. We know all families are at risk. Whether you are currently waging war or enjoying a time of peace, life will throw you curveballs. Like it or not, you'll be sucker punched.

Our apologies for being the bearers of bad news, but there it is. We also know that waiting until those curveballs break your nose makes recovery much more difficult. Why not learn to catch? We don't know if we would have listened had somebody handed us a book like this before Stuart's troubles began, but our hope is that at least some of you will. Please read with an open heart and allow these stories to teach and prepare you for what life has in store for your family!

# Life
# Happens

CHAPTER 1

# Define Family

**We are the Clarks,** a family of fifteen and counting. Our story begins like many others, with two people falling in love and choosing to build one life together. Teresa and Stuart were married July 3, 1980, and immediately began having their four wonderful children. Tiffany came first and now has a husband and four children of her own. Taralyn is the second oldest and loves to dote on her nieces and nephew. The third child is a boy, Steven, now married with two little ones. Taunalee brings up the caboose, and recently brought the next brave soul into our happy family when she married the man she has chosen to build a life with.

Ask anybody. Our family is close. We love spending time together and get along famously. We certainly have our share of conflicts and quirks, but we wouldn't change a thing. Those quirks make us who we are. We've been told countless times, "I love spending time with your family. It's like watching TV, only in real life!" We love this reputation. Our quick wits and loving jabs really do resemble a television sitcom.

For example, imagine us kneeling down for family prayer—an instant cue for each individual to suddenly become incredibly talkative and tell the family everything about their day. We usually end up rolling on the floor with laughter until Stuart becomes frustrated enough that he insists we calm down, ready to pray. "Steven, will you please say the prayer?" This question immediately spawns a light-hearted argument about whose turn it actually is to pray that night. After Steven returned home from his two-year church service mission to Germany, he was having a difficult time speaking English.

"Steven, will you please pray?"

"I don't remember how to pray in English!"

"Son, you may pray in whatever language you'd like."

Well, that did it. We all calmed down, and Steven began to pray in an unexpected language: Wookiee! Yes, Wookiee is the language that adorable fluff ball Chewbacca speaks in *Star Wars*. As you can imagine, this spun us into another fit of uncontrollable laughter, and it was at least another twenty minutes before the prayer was said. Welcome to the *Clark Show*!

Our favorite place to spend time together is the great outdoors. We grew up spending one to three weeks every year in Yellowstone National Park and the surrounding areas. Come rain or shine, you could find us in Yellowstone. We camped in tents in the summer, stayed in cabins and rode snow coaches into the park in the winter, took day trips to see the baby animals in the spring, and camped again in the fall when the tourists were mostly gone. We even drove through during the fires of 1988, with flames licking both sides of the highway. (Yes, we made a special trip for this.) Yellowstone was, and still is, our playground. When the kids were smaller, Teresa would read to the family from the aptly titled *Death in Yellowstone*. The book described exactly what you'd think: the unfortunate people who have died in Yellowstone and the many ways they perished. We all had favorite stories from the book that could be quoted verbatim. One of these was about a man who had fallen into a hot spring. When he emerged from the spring he was burned so badly that the outer layer of skin on his hands fell off like gloves.

Gruesome, but we loved it. And, rest assured, we had a deep respect for the power of Yellowstone. Teresa was able to stop leashing the kids after the book was found. And yes, the kids really did have leashes when they were younger. After all, people die in Yellowstone. As our family walked around the park, the kids would quote parts of their favorite stories:

"Mommy, isn't this the spring where that man's skin came off his hands like gloves?" "Why, yes, children it is. Well done."

Imagine the looks Teresa got from innocent bystanders! You just watched another episode of the *Clark Show*.

"Daddy all gone!" This unexpected comment from Teresa's three-year-old daughter in a canoe on the middle of Jackson Lake caught Teresa's attention right away. The family was in two canoes: Stuart had three-year-old Taunalee in the center of his canoe with ten-year-old Taralyn in the front, and Teresa had seven-year-old Steven and twelve-year-old Tiffany in her canoe. Taunalee (a.k.a. Taz) had gone with her father because she tended to wiggle excessively. Her placement in front of Stuart in the canoe gave him the opportunity to calm her down when she got too stirred up, or so he thought. Taunalee had become fascinated with the swirls the paddles made when they entered the water and had started bouncing from side to side to witness each paddle entry. That got the canoe rocking. It sounded like this to Teresa: "Taunalee! Stop! Ahhh!"

Splash. Teresa looked back just in time to see Stuart's hat floating to the surface, followed rapidly by Stuart's sputtering face. "There he is!" Taunalee declared with glee. Taralyn, completely oblivious to the drama unfolding in her canoe, just kept paddling. Stuart had taken quite a chilly dip; Jackson Lake rarely reaches sixty degrees Fahrenheit. The cold from falling into the water was intensified by the mountain-spring clothing he was wearing: long sleeves, jeans, and hiking boots.

This incident certainly could have gone bad quickly. However, Teresa's ability to remain calm in the midst of crisis helped both her and the children refrain from panicking. The biggest obstacle was getting Taralyn to stop paddling long enough for her father to reach and hang on to the side of the canoe. Once she became aware of her surroundings, we all made it safely to shore, wrung Stuart out as best as we could, then piled back into our canoes. Shortly thereafter the family escorted a soggy Stuart into a gift shop where he purchased a Grand Teton sweatshirt as the family laughed hysterically over the mishap. Imagine the looks that garnered, especially given the size of the puddle pooling up around Stuart's feet! We hope you enjoyed episode three of the *Clark Show*. Here comes episode four.

We have always enjoyed playing board and card games together. Killer Uno is a family favorite, a twist on regular Uno that's sure to keep you on your toes. Slow-paced games can be a little dangerous for our family, particularly if we're playing with individuals who take the game seriously. You see, we quickly get irritated with the pace of the game and figure out ways to speed things up. Monopoly with Grandma is a classic example. Grandma likes to win. We don't like Monopoly. The combination results in under-the-table deals between everybody at the game board except Grandma, who becomes so upset she's losing that she doesn't even recognize what's happening. We laugh hysterically and call the game a success! Not, mind you, because we won, but because we were entertained by the venture. You would have been, too. Later, when

Grandma accuses us of cheating, we let her know that nobody follows the rules in the real-life game of Monopoly. Rules are made to be broken; we were just making the game more realistic. Grandma remains upset about losing until she claims victory because we all cheated. Fair enough. Want to play a game?

Get ready for episode five.

"Why have four-wheel drive if we aren't going to use it?"

There was logic to the question. Besides, Stuart was ready with a map clearly showing the dirt roads he intended to take. Stuart loves maps because Stuart loves exploring. This man has no trust for a GPS device; he wants the paper in his hand with the data collected and printed by the U.S. Geological Survey clearly in front of him. If he has that map, he is pretty fearless.

Stuart, the explorer, planned to take his family on an adventure over some rarely-used, backcountry dirt roads in Utah that stretched from Strawberry Reservoir to Springville. Okay, sounded fun! He had the map and we had the new four-wheel drive vehicle, so what could possibly go wrong? This little drive along the Wasatch Range would take about an hour via state highways and the interstate. He estimated we were looking at approximately two hours on dirt roads. He was wrong. The rarely-used dirt roads had become overgrown in places and altered in others. There was even a fork in the road that never made the map. At one point, the intrepid explorer ended up driving down a creek bed that was marked as a road on the map.

He thought we were getting closer to our destination when a bend in that creek led us towards another car in the creek. There was an aged man behind the wheel and a silver-haired woman standing to the side of the car. We were getting close to civilization! We thought the woman was fishing until we saw her pull up her pants (so much for civilization). The funny thing was, our journey was nowhere near complete when we passed that couple. Four hours later, we arrived in Springville. Covered in mud and dirt and thrilled with our adventure, we were bursting to share the tale with others.

Road trips have always been a favorite family pastime. We have driven all over the country and seen some incredible things. Episode six of the *Clark Show* happens in our 1985 Volkswagen Vanagon, headed toward Texas for a family reunion. Our vacation destinations were usually the homes of extended family, and if they weren't, we stopped at their homes along the way. The trip to Texas was particularly memorable because the Vanagon had no air conditioning, and we were driving in August during the dead heat of the Texas summer.

You can ask anyone in our family about this road trip and hear one of two stories, after an exclamation of, "I hate Texas."

Rather than hearing about the fun activities we did once we arrived, you'll either hear about Taunalee's heat exhaustion or the cows. Teresa faithfully squirted each of the kids in the face with water mist from a spray bottle every thirty minutes, and the dashboard fan was going the whole time, but it wasn't quite enough for heat-sensitive Taunalee. After she deposited her previously consumed snacks into an empty dinosaur-fruit-snack box (all over Taralyn's lap), the family pulled over at a picnic area to clean up. This is the part of the story Taunalee will tell you.

Taralyn will tell you both the story of Taunalee's heat exhaustion and the cows, but Tiffany and Steven will only tell you about the cows. The kids had never seen longhorn steer before, and they walked toward the fence in fascination while waiting for Taunalee to cool down in the shade. As they did so, the herd of cattle turned in unison, ran a safe distance, and turned back in unison to stare down the perpetrators. The kids backed off long enough for the cows to come back to the fence, and then the cows ran at the kids again, achieving the same result. Synchronized stampede! This scene replayed itself over and over again, becoming funnier each time. We loved those cows. Cows in Idaho don't do that.

After Taunalee was sufficiently cool, we hopped back into the Vanagon to finish our journey and road trip games. This was before the days of TVs, DVD players, and video game consoles in cars. We had to entertain ourselves, and we were pretty good at it. Teresa read for hours on end, and Stuart taught the kids wonderfully irritating songs such as "Comet" and "Scab Salad" that Teresa barely tolerated. Also, the alphabet game would last forever, Klutz books occupied us, and there were, of course, plenty of complaints.

"He's breathing on me!" "She's in my space!" "I'm hungry. How much longer?" "He's looking out my window!" "Can I have some Twizzlers?" The Twizzlers were "driver stay awake" food, so no one could have any of those. Travel somewhere with one of the kid's families now, and you'll likely hear the same answer. Road trips were crazy and long, but they brought us close together and are definitely a huge part of who we are. Long road trips filled with Teresa's voice and Stuart's goofy jokes are stored among our favorite episodes of the *Clark Show*.

Clark family Christmas Eves have always been crammed full of traditions.

We visit family, sing carols, eat our traditional Christmas Eve feast, engage in age-old banter, act out the Nativity, and the kids all sleep in the same room because it is the only way any of them go to sleep. Christmas Eve has always been a production in our home. We know how Christmas Eve is supposed to go, and we throw fits if somebody tries to change it. We all recall with disgust a Christmas Eve dinner at Grandma and Grandpa Clark's home; they fed us bratwurst instead of our traditional spread. Christmas was ruined, and we've had ham ever since. In our home, guests become shepherds, grandparents become wise men, the unfortunate cat who dares wander through the living room for attention gets wrapped in quilt batting and becomes a lamb, and everyone gets matching pajamas. This annually repeated Christmas edition of the *Clark Show* never gets old.

Although we love adventures, most episodes of the *Clark Show* take place in our own home. When we're not road tripping, hiking, biking, canoeing, or camping, you can find us playing games, talking, laughing, watching movies, attending church services together, or cooking and eating together. The kids run to Stuart when he gets home from work, and everyone ends up on the floor in a family mountain. We gather in the family room in our pajamas on New Year's Day for a movie marathon. Stuart plays the piano or Teresa sits in the hallway and reads to the kids as they fall asleep. We eat dinner together as a family, study the scriptures, and say our prayers. We talk about and relish in individual and family accomplishments. We talk about the hard things in life and comfort those experiencing them. We remind each other who we are as a family and what we value. We double as each other's best friends, and it shows! We are the Clarks: an outdoorsy, God-fearing, fun-and-food-loving, tradition-keeping, loud, crazy, and active family. Or at least we were.

# Meet the Tidlunds

"Taralyn, is this the hot pot where that man's skin came off his hands like gloves?"

"Why yes, Madison, it is."

"I want to come here every year so that when I have kids I can tell them about Yellowstone, and it will be a childhood memory for me like it is for you and my mom."

Tiffany married Bryan Tidlund on June 1, 2001. It wasn't long before they had four wonderful children: Hadley, Madison, Katelyn, and Colter. The Tidlund family is a lot like the Clark family because Tiffany carried many of our traditions into her marriage. The family still goes on epic adventures, practices many of the same Christmas traditions, and tells some of the same stories. Bryan brought his traditions into the Tidlund family as well. So although they are similar to the Clarks, they are definitely their own breed.

The Tidlunds love spending time together as a family and can most often be found doing just that. Their favorite activities are outside activities such as camping, hiking, shooting, playing on four-wheelers, gardening, going on family walks, swimming, or just playing in their backyard. If the family is stuck inside, you can find them watching a movie together, having a dance party in the living room, playing their newest Wii game, cooking and eating meals together, playing games together, or going for drives.

Tiffany and Bryan moved six times during the first decade of their marriage, so the Tidlunds are accustomed to long car rides to visit fun tourist spots and faraway family members. They have now settled closer to Bryan's parents and Tiffany's parents and spend much of their free time visiting extended family members so their children will know their grandparents, aunts, uncles, and cousins. Bryan works hard to support the family, and Tiffany stays home to care for the children. They are also a religious family and attend church services on a weekly basis. Meet the Tidlunds: a family-focused, outdoorsy, faithful, trusting, spontaneous, silly, and fearless family. Or at least they were.

Many diverse and varied families outside of our own family have shared their stories with us as we have worked toward completing this project. Their stories are both powerful and valuable in further understanding how families can maintain family strength and unity in the face of adversity.

# Meet the Crandalls

Marcus and Julie were happily married and soon had their beautiful daughter Kassie. They chose to move away from their parents to fulfill their shared desire to build their own traditions and identity. Julie was threatened by Marcus's relationship with his mother and felt they needed distance to assure that Julie and Marcus's relationship came first. Julie came from a family with a history of anxiety and difficulty with anger management and wanted to ensure the pattern did not repeat itself in her new family. Marcus and Julie were happy with the plan and the location where they had landed, far away from extended family. They kept in touch with extended family through phone calls and emails as they began their own little family.

Marcus and Julie were both very career minded. While Marcus finished his career training, Julie worked hard to support the family. She also worked hard to help Marcus with his schooling. Marcus had struggled with school studies since his teens. Julie had patiently helped him work through his struggles once they were married. For the first time in his life, Marcus was thriving in an educational setting and had the grades to prove it. There wasn't a lot of time for extracurricular play, but they enjoyed biking and watching movies together when they could snatch a few moments. Marcus spoke Spanish and wanted his family to be bilingual as well, so they also watched a lot of Spanish game shows on TV.

Kassie came along just as Marcus was finishing up his education. As a result, much of Kassie's first year was actually spent with Marcus. He reveled in being a husband and father and enjoyed having Kassie looking snappy and having dinner on the table when Julie got home from work. After Marcus entered his full-time career, Julie came home to be the caregiver. Her parental focus was on quality play and learning. She was not nearly as interested in a clean home or consistent dinner hour as Marcus had been, but Kassie thrived under Julie's constant attention and influence. At two she had the vocabulary and imagination of a child much older than her. And that's when everything changed.

# Meet the Kellers

"When I think of our family, the first word that comes to mind is 'crazy' or 'wild,'" says Sam Keller. Perhaps the nine children running around their home creates this perception. On a typical day, the family gets up early to study the scriptures together and runs out the door. The day is spent with Sam at work, the majority of the kids at school, and Shayna busily taking care of their home. She also serves as a taxi driver for the kids and runs errands.

When Sam gets home from work, he immediately drops his work things and wrestles with the boys in the front room so Shayna and the girls can have time and space to prepare dinner. Dinner is served, evening sports and church events consume the remainder of the day, and the Kellers go to bed ready to do it all over again the next day.

Sam and Shayna both came from large families and wanted a large family of their own. They got it! They've been blessed with nine beautiful children: three girls and six boys, each with unique personalities and interests that keep their parents guessing. They are an intelligent and creative family, excelling at all they do and constantly creating meals and experiments together, often leaving chaos in their wake. Incidentally, family birthdays and holiday celebrations are an enormous production, chock-full of elaborate traditions and huge feasts.

During the summer months, you'll find the Kellers outside camping, hiking, playing sports, or just goofing around in the backyard. Shayna explains that they are family focused and have "always had a strong family ethic and . . . the desire to have [the kids] at the center of [their] lives." This shows in the way their family is always together, supporting one another in challenges and pursuits. They are also a religious and service-oriented family, always striving to reach out to those less fortunate, never expecting to be the family needing others to reach out to them.

# Meet the Zales

Lorena and Matthew Zale said "I do" on ice in their hockey skates and Victorian-style clothing. What a first wedding for the mayor of their city to perform! The family proudly embraces Lorena's Irish Catholic heritage, Matthew's Russian Jewish heritage, and the African American heritage of their adopted son. Although they are proud of their heritage, the different ways in which Lorena and Matthew were raised definitely presented some challenges.

In spite of the diversity, Lorena and Matthew meant their marriage vows and have found ways to make everything work. They both are service oriented and love spending time with handicapped children. Their own son came from an abusive home and has some learning disabilities, yet they have embraced the challenge by providing their son a loving and supportive home environment. They also work hard to maintain ties with his biological family. Stories of the Zales' heritage strengthen familial ties while stories of family vacations and adventures help create a sense of love and belonging in their home. Matthew is in his second marriage and is twenty years older than Lorena and never would have guessed how things would turn out for their little family.

# Meet the Goodsons

Richard would tell you that he married a ready-made family. It was Sarah's second marriage, and she brought two children from her first marriage. Richard and Sarah then had one additional child, resulting in a total of three. They met at a bar and fell in love while dancing, though their values have since changed. Sarah became active in her church while Richard served in the navy for twenty-one years, and he eventually became a baptized member of her faith.

Though their lifestyle is now different, they continue to share a love of dancing, camping, playing board games, being silly with their family, and building new traditions such as snowmobiling and scouting. They are a health-conscious, service-oriented, and orderly family. Richard and Sarah saw themselves dancing through life together, never dreaming the dancing would have to stop.

# Meet the Clowards

When Justin first tried asking his wife Jessica on a date, she misunderstood the question and set him up with her friend instead. Through Justin's persistence, Jessica finally listened and eventually accepted his marriage proposal. Five children later, the couple remains happily married. Jessica was determined to be an incredible mother and spent much of her time reading and researching how to do just that. Family stories were often used to teach the value of persistence, good communication, and other life skills. The Clowards fiercely support each other and are proud of one another's accomplishments. No matter whom you ask in the family, a list of family members automatically comes with a list of degrees earned and personal triumphs.

The family enjoys playing board games together and sharing fond memories of family vacations to faraway places. They are lovers of learning, perhaps in part due to Jessica's efforts in reading to and teaching them when they were younger. The Clowards were comfortable with each other and kept to themselves for the most part, never imagining they would later face the trial that would teach them the value of community.

# Meet the Swintons

Kari's first marriage ended in divorce, though she was blessed with two wonderful children from that marriage. Adam worked hard to build relationships with his new wife and two stepchildren, taking them on camping adventures and participating in large family barbeques in the backyard on holidays and other special occasions. The children, particularly the daughter, missed their biological father and didn't make it easy for Adam to fit in. He admits he doesn't always work at building and maintaining those relationships as hard as he should and turns to alcohol to deaden some of the emotions his newfound family life creates.

Kari remains dedicated to her children and counts motherhood as one of her greatest responsibilities and blessings no matter the difficulties inherent in that role. She works hard to support her nearly grown children and keep her marriage with Adam alive, but the situation tends to change when the supporter becomes the person needing support.

# Meet the Franklins

The Franklins believe one person's problem is the entire family's problem, and they illustrate this belief by rallying around each other, much like buffalo or elk rally around their calves when a pack of wolves comes prowling. Jennifer and her husband were blessed with three beautiful daughters. Many of their family traditions involve stories of family history and lessons learned from those stories. Jennifer hosts "Grandma's Day" every summer in an effort to establish and maintain meaningful relationships with each of her grandchildren. No parents allowed.

They spend the holidays together and are a deeply religious and service-oriented family, making their church service and religious practices central in their lives. They would all tell you they have a loving and close family. Perhaps this is the reason they've been able to remain loving and close despite some of the trials that commonly tear other families to pieces.

# Define Family

We often find ourselves in situations away from family, and some people don't even have family to be separated from. In such situations, the term family becomes a little more elastic. Taralyn worked at a wilderness rehabilitation program for at-risk youth and saw alternative families established time and again.

After a long, hard day of hiking, groups of at-risk youth just wanted to get the fire going, wrap up dinner, and get into bed. This wasn't always possible. After such a day, one group began digging a fire pit with no success. Already exhausted, the group did not find the frozen and unyielding ground a laughing matter, but Taralyn laughed anyway. What a perfect ending to an already grueling day! Though she laughed in frustration at the irony of the situation, the kids in her group that week saw more in her laugh than she realized.

Once the fire was lit and the day was finally coming to a close, one young man looked at her and said, "I like the way you laugh all the time. It's something about your laugh . . . it calmed me down. I knew everything would be ok." Taralyn was surprised as all of the students and staff surrounding the fire nodded in agreement. These experiences brought groups close together, and they became families: fiercely protecting each other, relishing in each other's accomplishments, bickering like siblings, and expressing anger when others made poor decisions. Similar situations play out in boarding schools and orphanages around the world.

Everywhere you turn for a definition of family, you will find something new and different, a definition often contrary to the definition you just read. The truth is that family is different for everybody. Adults may be married, divorced, widowed, or unwed; children may have one parent, two parents, foster parents, adoptive and biological parents, or no parents at all. No matter the makeup of a family, no matter your definition, family strength and unity come in consistent and predictable ways. No matter the depth of your family's strength and unity, a sucker punch is on its way. Will you be ready?

# CHAPTER 2

# Sucker Punched

Our active world came crashing to a halt in 2007 when Stuart's chronic roller coaster achieved permanent status. Although the doctors tell us things began in 2007, we can look back and identify a key moment that triggered the slow fade of Stuart's health.

"Teresa!" It had been a normal New Year's Day in the Clark house. We had stayed in our pajamas all day long, enjoying hours upon hours of a *Star Wars* movie marathon. Now night was upon us, and we were getting ready to shift back into the routines school and work require. Stuart had stepped outside to put new windshield wipers on the car. "Teresa!" She was on the phone and didn't hear Stuart screaming her name. He was screaming her name at the top of his lungs; he never screams. Taralyn thought she heard Stuart yelling outside but wasn't sure. She got up and began walking toward the front door. "Mom, I think Dad's screaming your name." She reached the front porch just as Stuart did. Looking down, he grimaced and said, "I think I broke my ankle. What do you think?"

Stuart had stepped outside without a coat on. It was bitterly cold, but there was no snow to speak of. The driveway was clear except for one little patch of ice, no bigger than a five-by-seven-inch index card. Stuart's left foot hit the edge of that patch of ice and slid across it with enough speed that when his foot hit the dry pavement on the opposite side, his body was not prepared to stop. The momentum of that slide focused and compounded with great force as his ankle took the entire brunt of the fall.

Taralyn looked down and saw that Stuart's ankle was positioned ninety degrees to the right of where it should have been. Teresa was off the phone now. A long night at the hospital followed. On the drive there, Stuart said he'd just dislocated his ankle; the hospital staff would pop it back in, and he'd be back to work the next morning. Teresa didn't actually hear the words, but she felt them with absolute certainty: "No, he won't." The week prior to New Year's had been spent at Stuart's parents house. His father, LaMar, was dying. Not everyone in the extended family was acknowledging that fact yet, but we knew it. We'd spent the week putting on a happy face for everyone else, posing for family pictures while knowing they would be our last with LaMar and planning for a future we knew would not include LaMar.

Coming home had been grueling because of what we were leaving behind, but it was such a relief to be home where we were free to be ourselves and face the future honestly. Prior to Stuart's fall we had started focusing on what would be needed for the following day. School routines and work schedules loomed. Teresa had just started a new phase of a college home-study program and needed to figure out how to make that fit into already busy routines.

As Teresa stood in the emergency room watching a litany of doctors and nurses care for Stuart, she had an overwhelming feeling wash over her that things were much more complicated than she and Stuart had assumed. One steel plate and several screws later, Stuart was in the recovery room. Teresa was told the surgery had gone well but that Stuart was looking at six weeks with no weight on his foot. Six weeks off from work. Six weeks of home health care. Six weeks of balancing Stuart's crisis with the fact his father was dying hundreds of miles away. While Teresa was being told about how quickly Stuart would heal, doctors were having a hard time waking him up in the recovery room. His oxygen dropped to incredibly low levels; his breathing stopped. Everyone became anxious. Long after Teresa was supposed to have seen Stuart again, he remained in recovery. Teresa quite clearly remembers having a conversation with God as she waited. It was obvious to her that life was taking an interesting turn. She prayed for peace, and she prayed for strength. The ankle break didn't cause Stuart's new problem: chronic illness was a slow fade. In truth, we still had some time before we would even use the words chronic illness, but the surgery and the hospitalization opened the door to the reality that all was not right in Stuart's world. All was not right in our family's world.

All the kids were still living at home in 1998. Tiffany and Taralyn were in high school, Steve was in middle school, and Taunalee was in elementary school. The changes in Stuart's health were so gradual that we all remember it differently. Some of us were shocked with the doctor's diagnosis of Dad's chronic problems in 2007, while others were relieved to finally know the root of the problem. There was one thing we all knew, though: our identity was in danger. There was no possible way we were going to let his life-threatening illnesses and resulting complications get the best of our family. We continued doing everything we had always done, sometimes dragging Stuart along for the ride. We were still the Clarks: an outdoorsy, God-fearing, fun-loving, tradition-keeping, food-loving, loud, crazy, and active family.

Between 2007 and the writing of this book in 2013, Stuart has had twelve major surgeries, been diagnosed and treated for three rare diseases, dealt with bleeding ulcers, undergone several invasive medical procedures, received over twenty-five different long-term prescription medications, experienced countless medicinal complications and withdrawals, and more. Taunalee was the only child left at home when things really became complicated. Steve and Tiffany had both found spouses and started their own families; Taralyn had graduated college and was working out of state at a wilderness rehabilitation facility for at-risk youth; and Taunalee was in high school. In short, the man Taunalee grew up with is not the man Tiffany, Taralyn, and Steve grew up with.

Taralyn became a bridge between the adult children and Taunalee when she got a local job and moved back home in 2007. This was a conscious decision to provide emotional and physical support for her parents and younger sibling in crisis. It placed her on the frontlines of this battle and gave her the role of witness. Unbeknownst to her, this choice would also lead her forward to a master's thesis on the influence of chronic illness on family relationships and leisure patterns and would steer her professional career choices.

We have a family rule we feel very strongly about, a rule we're about to break. After all, if we learn anything from the game of Monopoly, it is that rules are meant to be broken as long as the majority benefits. The rule is this: don't keep score. In other words, it is not wise to look back and count up all your trials, sorrows, and pain. It is not wise to wallow through your pet sufferings again and again. It is not wise to compare your trials to the trials of others. We are big advocates for living one day at a time and looking forward. That being said, we need to tally up the score. We do not do this to suggest we have suffered more or dealt with more than you have. We have heard enough stories to know our situation is not unique or even extraordinary. We do it only to emphasize our familiarity with curveballs. We have dodged a few and have been sucker punched by a few as well. We share the score to set the stage.

In the course of a single decade, our extended family experienced its share of transitional upheavals. While our life upheavals started with Stuart shattering his ankle and continued to be laced with his ongoing medical challenges, it was also rife with other shakeups. Compiled into one list, the challenges can seem breathtaking. Brace yourself.

During that decade we lost both of Stuart's parents to cancer, Teresa had a heart attack (Did you know spouses of chronically ill individuals are fifty times more likely to have a heart attack and experience other health problems?), Stuart received an unexpected 30 percent cut in pay that necessitated a job change, Teresa entered the workforce to ease the burden of Stuart's job change, and we moved twice. Our family spread over great distances in several states as all of the kids graduated from high school and moved on to college, and two of the kids were married and became parents. One of the kids experienced numerous pregnancy complications including a heartbreaking miscarriage. Three of the kids did some substantial traveling in Europe, China, the United States, and Ecuador. One served a two-year church service mission in Germany. In the course of those two years, Taralyn walked over a thousand miles and spent over 360 days and nights working with at-risk youth in a wilderness rehabilitation setting.

Teresa's mother experienced a life-threatening brain aneurysm, and her father battled cancer. One granddaughter developed a brain tumor, which was magnified by the fact that her great-grandfather had died from a brain tumor and her great-grandmother was losing her battle with cancer (culminating with the cancer metastasizing to her brain). Emergency surgery took place in one state while her great-grandmother passed away in another. Well, you get the idea. It's best not to keep score.

# The Tidlunds

"Is a CAT scan really necessary?"

Tiffany was certain seven-year-old Hadley's headaches were the result of dehydration or stress from their recent move, but she reluctantly took her in to see a new pediatrician. By now, Tiffany was a well-seasoned mother of three and was familiar with this frustrating line: "There's nothing we can do. You'll just have to take her home and give it time." Her mother confirmed her belief that the CAT scan was probably overkill if Hadley was only experiencing occasional headaches, even if they were severe. Bryan felt differently, and so the CAT scan was scheduled for a few weeks after Hadley's initial doctor visit.

Hadley felt fine and was acting normally on the day of the CAT scan. She was a little nervous but calmed down once Tiffany explained the doctors would just be taking a picture of her brain. Tiffany and Hadley sat laughing and teasing as they waited to hear the results of the test. As soon as Tiffany saw the look on the radiologist's face, the laughing and teasing was over for her, though Hadley was confused and didn't understand what was going on or why her mother was crying. She wouldn't stop crying.

When the two arrived home, Tiffany and Bryan put on a movie for their three daughters, then cried and held each other until the phone call came from Hadley's pediatrician. Hadley was diagnosed with a brain tumor, a juvenile pilocytic astrocytoma, three centimeters in diameter. Emergency surgery was required, and she had already been admitted to the children's hospital in a nearby city.

Tiffany and Bryan scrambled to find somebody to watch and care for their other two children for an undetermined amount of time. All of their extended family was far away and unable to help due to weather conditions and the fact that Tiffany's grandma was dying in another state. They felt utterly alone. What would Hadley's fate be? This was the third brain tumor diagnosis in the family, and the previous two did not end well. Tiffany and Bryan left their two youngest daughters in the hands of people they barely knew from their new church congregation and headed for the hospital, brimming over with worry, doubt, loneliness, and fear.

# The Crandalls

Kassie didn't look sick, but Marcus and Julie knew something was not quite right. Kassie's energy levels were slightly off and her happy temperament kept giving way to unexpected tantrums. Of course, Kassie was two years old, so weren't tantrums to be expected? She tired easily, took progressively longer naps, and seemed to be bruised all the time. When the twinkle in her eye began to fade, her parents finally took her in to see the doctor. The devastating news was preceded by a series of tests and a lot of anxious waiting; Kassie had leukemia.

It was as if a nuclear explosion had taken place, and they were at ground zero. The diagnosis changed everything. Gone were the days of bikes and kites in the park. Gone were the evenings spent cuddled together as a family. Kassie's diagnosis resulted in countless treatments in the hospital, spinal taps, chemotherapy, sleepless nights, fear, and rapidly mounting medical bills. Marcus took on more and more shifts at work, sometimes working twenty hours in a day. Julie spent hours learning all she could about how to care for and feed such a sick little girl. She also took on the full brunt of Kassie's treatments, some of which kept Kassie in the hospital for two to three weeks at a time.

Extended family started taking turns traveling to be with the devastated family and help during the weeks of hospitalization. Everyone felt fear not only for Kassie's long-term outlook, but also for the long-term outlook of the family. Marcus and Julie were rarely together anymore. They slept and lived on completely different schedules. Extended family encouraged them to make time for their relationship. They sent them out on dates and made sure they met with hospital counselors. Marcus and Julie were warned by professionals that divorce rates for parents of critically ill children were dangerously high. Marcus and Julie appreciated the help, but not the advice.

# The Kellers

Sam Keller was experiencing sinus problems severe enough to be cutting into his well-being and productivity. He felt amazing after his first sinus surgery, though it only took a few days for him to feel worse than ever. He no longer had the energy to wrestle with his boys, spend time with his family in the evenings, hike and camp in tents, work in the yard or garage, or finish home remodeling projects. The childcare and home responsibilities fell unexpectedly and completely on Shayna's shoulders. Sam's health even influenced his ability to work, and Shayna had to step in there as well.

Increased stress at home led to the three eldest children acting out (anorexia, attempted suicide) in attempts to get more of the attention they had lost. Also, Sam's eventual diagnosis of chronic fatigue syndrome and fibromyalgia led to continued surgeries, never-ending pain, expensive prescription medications, and a reconstruction of home life. The family became so focused on caring for and protecting themselves that previous leisure pursuits, traditions, and individual needs and wants fell by the wayside.

# The Zales

Matthew remembers Lorena always dealing with chronic pain from migraines and endometriosis. Their son Jared can't remember her ever being well. Her real trouble began shortly after Jared was adopted; she had a hysterectomy and a bad case of West Nile virus. She never really healed, and the chronic pain and seemingly endless list of symptoms and diagnoses is alarming.

Suddenly, Matthew found himself in the role of a single dad as he took on all of Lorena's responsibilities in addition to his own. She was twenty years younger, and he always imagined she would be the one taking care of him. Nevertheless, her constant pain and fatigue reversed their roles in the blink of an eye. Lorena is now homebound, unable to participate in previously enjoyed sporting activities, camping trips, and family vacations. She is no longer able to work, and she misses rocking the babies that brought her so much peace and joy. When you ask Lorena what her illness is called, she will provide a long list of troubles, including fibromyalgia and chronic fatigue syndrome. When you ask the Zales about Lorena's prognosis, you won't hear anything positive. They know they are in it for the long haul.

# The Goodsons

Sarah and Richard were thrilled with the birth of their first child together, the third child in their blended family. Shortly after Aaron was born, Sarah's battle with chronic fatigue syndrome began, though it wouldn't be called that for years to come. If you look at her medical charts, you still won't find a diagnosis because she's afraid she wouldn't be able to afford insurance if she ever had to switch companies. Sarah's symptoms came on slowly and initially looked like recovery from childbirth.

Aaron's birth seemed to trigger the chronic nature of her illness, and he grew up with a different mom than the older two children did. He recalls moments of normalcy with her; though most memories involve her just watching because participating would wear her out for days, even weeks, to come. Sarah often requires long afternoon naps, experiences difficulties completing everyday tasks, and can't be as active as she was in the past. Sarah states her illness has become "an everyday awareness" and prevents her from doing many things she loves doing, though the activity she misses most is dancing with her sweetheart.

# The Clowards

Jessica's diagnosis of fibromyalgia took the Cloward family by storm. She can tell you the exact date and time when she realized she would never be the same. She lay on the couch shortly after her hysterectomy and realized the pain would never go away. The realization and resulting diagnosis spun her into a yearlong bout with severe depression. She was unable to engage in activities she loved or contribute to family life in meaningful ways. Her depression resulted in suicidal thoughts that terrified her husband and child still living at home. As Jessica battled depression, her teenage daughter Sharon took on many of her mother's responsibilities, caring for the home and her mother as if her mother were the child. Jessica's husband Justin explains, "Until you've personally experienced the chronic pain you can't understand it." Jessica explains it best: it's like putting clothespins on every square inch of your body, knowing that pain and discomfort will never go away. Now you might be able to understand what it's like to live with fibromyalgia.

# The Swintons

"Kari, are you ok?"

She had taken a pretty hard fall at a work party, and her coworkers were concerned. This fall was not normal behavior for Kari. Numerous tests and doctor visits resulted in a diagnosis of multiple sclerosis, a typically progressive nerve disease that causes permanent damage which can result in difficulty balancing, memory loss, and chronic fatigue and pain. Kari was experiencing all of these symptoms, though you wouldn't guess it from her attitude.

Kari kept a smile on her face and did her best to make things look normal, though her illness was seeping into her life in ways she couldn't control. Her relationships with her husband and children became strained, and Adam began drinking alcohol more frequently with friends while spending less time at home. Her mother came around more to help out when Adam should have been helping, but it was difficult for Kari to accept her mother's help. Kari's children didn't know how to help their mother, which was a source of frustration for them. It was easier to not be home. The family seemed more like a collection of individuals sharing a roof than an actual family.

# The Franklins

In the midst of experiencing chronic pain and severe depression, Jennifer was undergoing a psychiatric assessment behind closed doors when she received a note from her husband, which read "I don't love you anymore. I want a divorce." With the divorce final, Jennifer received her diagnosis of fibromyalgia and rapidly lost her job as she became unable to work and ineligible to receive unemployment benefits.

Jennifer went from being married and working full time to being a single mom who was dependent on her children for financial support as she faced the fear and uncertainty that comes hand-in-hand with a diagnosis of chronic illness. Her constant pain resulted in difficulties focusing and intolerance for noisy situations, therefore impacting her ability to engage in community endeavors, leisure pursuits, and family relationships. She felt she was a failure in many ways and turned to her only source of peace: religion.

# Other "Families"

"No, don't go!"

It took everything Taralyn had to pry little Austin off of her arm and run from the orphanage, leaving him screaming in tears behind her. When she got around the corner her own tears were like waterfalls running down her face. She had seen Austin and all of the orphans nearly every day for the past three months as she volunteered at this orphanage. They captured her heart. As she paused to catch her breath, she could still hear them crying and screaming her name. For a split second, she wondered why she kept doing this to herself: volunteering at boarding schools and orphanages in foreign countries, only to love and then leave her little angels. Another scene replayed in her mind of the bus she and other volunteers were on when it pulled away from the boarding school as children lined the sides of the bus, crying and running after it. In moments like this it felt more like torture than loving service.

"So, how did you come to a wilderness therapy program?" was a common question among the at-risk teens Taralyn worked with. A large majority of them had no idea they were headed to a wilderness rehabilitation program until they were picked up. The stories were all the same. "I was woken up in the middle of the night by this huge dude who tackled me. He cuffed me and dragged me screaming out to his car. My parents were crying, but they don't care about me. If they cared they wouldn't have sent me here." This is really what happened. Most parents would hire an escort service to pick up their child in the middle of the night when they knew they would actually be home and in bed. The escort service deposited them at the program, where they were tested for drugs, given their gear, blindfolded, and driven out into the wilderness. Within a period of twenty-four hours, most kids went from sleeping comfortably at home in their beds to being dropped off in the middle of nowhere with no idea of what the future held.

Welcome to the wilderness. No, you may not ask questions pertaining to the future; live in the present. No, you may not talk about your past with other group members. You get no phone calls; we don't have phones. Staff members will screen your letters. You will be given clothing that is identical to the clothing everyone else is wearing. You will hike every day, come rain or shine, no matter the season. You will learn to make fire with nothing but sticks or you won't eat warm meals or progress through the program. Don't worry; you'll like it here! We're like family.

It doesn't matter what your family looks like; every family gets sucker punched. Hopefully these stories help you realize just how normal your family really is! No matter what ails your family, rest assured other families fight similar battles. Chronic illness, divorce, the blending of different cultures, adoption and orphanage, substance abuse and addiction, the death of loved ones, various forms of abuse, and other ailments plague families the world over. Where exactly is normal in all of this? We would submit normal is what we experience in the midst of change and trial.

We have come to accept sucker punches as quests. There is a choice with the arrival of each new challenge. You can throw up your hands in despair and perish or hold on tight and survive. If you choose to survive, you can learn to succeed and even thrive in the midst of change; however, success is not possible unless you clearly see what you are dealing with and open your eyes to the people all around you.

# CHAPTER 3

# Tunnel Vision

"Paddle or die." That's what the river guide said to us when she put us in the front of the raft. Class three and four rapids laced between towering pine trees and looming canyon walls make running the Salmon River the thrill of a lifetime. We chuckled at the river guide's instruction, as we tend to do at inappropriate times. She grabbed our arms. "Teresa, Taralyn, I'm serious. It's up to you two to get us through this alive." Suddenly the phrase "river of no return" took on deadly meaning. The fast-moving current makes for a marvelous river run, though it is nearly impossible to return upstream once you begin your journey; the river of no return is how people have referred to the Salmon River for centuries.

We anticipated a crazy fun wild ride, but the two of us did not anticipate rowing for our lives. We had been assigned to a raft containing four other passengers and our river guide. The teenage boys had initially been placed in the front of the raft because they declared they were "experienced rafters." The moms in their late forties had been placed at the back of the raft because they were "along for the ride." We were placed in the middle, where we would need to paddle, but "not do all the work." That all changed when we dipped into our first class-four rapid with the back of the raft facing downstream. The boys were screaming in fear, the river guide was yelling at everyone to paddle harder, the moms were ashen and stunned to silence, and we were paddling with all our might.

It was clear something needed to change in a hurry. There was no turning back; the current made that painfully obvious. The steep cliff walls lining the river and the active forest fire on the trees above blocked our escape so that there would be no climbing out of the canyon. The only way to get off the river was to ride the raft to the landing ten miles downstream. The river guide steered us to the narrow shore along the river, livid at those "experienced" boys who had lied and put us all in jeopardy. That's when we offered to shift to the front. It wasn't a noble gesture; we just wanted to control our own destinies at that point. We wanted to get out alive.

Falling into that class-four rapid backwards was quite the sucker punch. In that moment of decision, we knew the risks of failure and decided failure was not an option, so we met the challenge. We rose up, dusted ourselves off, rolled up our sleeves, and accepted the quest presented. During our river run, we learned very quickly that tunnel vision is required when you are in the rapids. In order to know what kind of steering and paddling is required, you can't stop looking downriver for the next haystack, strainer, or pool drop. You simply don't have the privilege to take in the view, at least until you reach calm waters. You can't take a moment to lift your paddle and rest in the middle of the rapids. You can't look back. All you can do is paddle and trust your river guide to steer the safest route. During that run down the river, nothing else matters. Just keep your mouth shut, paddle, and listen and respond instantly for the next called out counsel of the river guide.

That's how we felt when everything went crazy with Stuart's health. In no time at all he had multiple surgeries and was taking an astounding amount of medication. We kept it to ourselves. Nobody could possibly understand our situation or see what we saw. Chronic illness looks different than many other setbacks. It's not a sudden tragedy. The sufferer may still look normal, and the world sees what they have always seen. Stuart has a unique work schedule; he works seven 10-hour shifts in a row and then has seven days off. In the beginning, we were able to schedule all of his medical procedures at the beginning of his off weeks. It was our little secret, our little cross to bear. No one saw the exhaustion, the altered routines, the simmering frustration and fear of the unknown, or the temptation to give in to hopelessness. In our stubborn pride, we believed that was the way we wanted it to be. No one needed to know our business, right? After all, we were tough. We are the Clarks, and we are fighters. We could and would maintain our identity.

So what did we do? We dragged him around, trying to keep up appearances. We even took him to an amusement park just two days after surgery. Our entire extended family would be there, and we felt he should be too. The poor guy sat in a camp chair in the corner of a pavilion for most of the day, feeling miserable. Since we weren't offering full disclosure of our situation, few of the extended family understood why he was so withdrawn. Mostly, they thought he was just being lazy.

And of course we took him camping! In our tenacious fight to maintain our identity, Taralyn, Taunalee, and Teresa announced they were hauling Stuart to the woods. Forget how tired he was. Forget what he couldn't do. We were fully capable of doing it all, and he could be miserable anywhere. We reasoned the fresh air would do him good. We were in total denial. We never stopped to think about how difficult it would be for him to get up in the middle of the night when sleeping on the ground. We never stopped to consider the impact high altitude would have on his weakened lungs. We never stopped to think about how dismissed he might feel when we turned him into luggage. We never stopped to think we might wound his pride if we pushed him around our favorite trails in a wheelchair.

We loaded him up like a puppy in a kennel and away we went. In our effort to maintain the status quo we disenfranchised the very person we were trying to maintain normalcy for.

For Taunalee's senior trip, we hauled Stuart off for another adventure. He was exhausted and cranky until we rented a Segway for him to enjoy our tour of some botanical gardens. Suddenly, he was completely free. He zoomed all over those gardens and left us in the dust. The smile on his face was incredible. We hadn't seen that smile for years. We dubbed him "Segway Man" and gave in to pure delight as we piled in a golf cart and chased him for hours all over those gardens. That's when our tunnel vision first began to fade.

Suddenly we realized we could be the same Clarks and enjoy the same activities. It would take some understanding, openness, and adaptation on our part, but our core values and beliefs were the same. This was not about us being caregivers and he being the one cared for. This was about us finding ways to help one another and exploring options for new avenues of joy and adventure. This was about honoring Stuart as the leader and patriarch of our family rather than treating him like a pet. This was about opening up to new options, receiving help from others, and extending help to others. We did not need to do this alone, nor could we.

# The Tidlunds

Tiffany and Bryan experienced tunnel vision before Hadley's tumor was ever diagnosed: "We never thought this would happen to our family." It was incredibly difficult for them to believe their firstborn child could have a problem requiring a CAT scan and emergency surgery, with years of follow-up MRIs and doctor visits. The realization hit them hard. Before letting anyone know what was wrong, they withdrew from their parents and children and spent time together as a couple processing what was happening in their lives.

The speed with which Hadley's surgery and recovery progressed required them to reach out for support earlier on, and their children required explanations about what was happening with Hadley and what her surgery and recovery would mean for their family. Their tunnel vision didn't last for long, but they did experience it. Ultimately, their eyes were forced open as they worked to find caregivers for their other two children throughout the ordeal. They could not do it alone.

# The Crandalls

As Kassie's treatments extended over weeks and months, Marcus and Julie grew further apart. Not only did the distance grow between the two of them but also between themselves and their extended family. It was all well and good for family to sashay in and help for a week or two, but the never-ending marital and family counsel was beginning to wear on the two of them. After all, they had purposefully moved far enough away to ensure extended family would not be privy to their daily affairs. Because of Kassie's illness, the whole family was more involved in their lives than they had ever wanted. Rather than feeling lifted and cared for, they felt oppressed.

Oh, they were deeply grateful for the family who would come and stay in the hospital with Kassie so they could be freed to accomplish other things, but they weren't as pleased when the family insisted on staying another week with them to continue to help out. "No, there's no need for you to come to our home. We're fine. We just need some space." They began to put up barriers. No one could possibly understand their relationship or their challenges by merely visiting for a week. Everyone's behavior was strained by such a situation anyway. Why couldn't they just be left alone?

# The Kellers

Shayna Keller explains how an outsider can't recognize that Sam faces the consequences of illness on a daily basis. Society suggests if you can't see something, it's not real. Sam wanted to keep his troubles private anyway. He had heard friends and family espouse beliefs that people with ailments like his are just lazy. He admitted to believing this himself at one point in his life. Others have said such trials come as a result of horrific sins committed. He didn't want others to view him or his family this way.

Shayna is aware of another family in their neighborhood in a similar situation. One of the parents has a progressive illness resulting in disability. Because she is in a wheelchair and community members can see the progression, they have rallied around the family in love and support. Nobody can see Sam's illness, so Shayna believes nobody will support her family in the same way. To the outside viewer, they must look chaotic and out of control. Besides, how do you tell somebody about something like this? No, it's easier to plow through it and get past it. Accepting it feels too much like giving up on Sam's ability to overcome hard things. It feels too much like giving up on the family.

# The Zales

Matthew wouldn't accept Lorena's problems as serious at first. They continued their normal routines until he could no longer deny the reality of their situation. They had gone out to eat at a local restaurant, and Lorena was literally falling asleep at the table. It had been a normal day, but the illness had just sapped all of the energy from her body. Reality sank in. Something was definitely wrong.

Doctors didn't help when she would tell them her symptoms and test after test would come back negative. "Are you sure you aren't a drug addict trying to get more pills?" It was harder for both Lorena and Matthew to accept her illness when everyone around them doubted her symptoms. To this day, Lorena doesn't have a certain diagnosis. How can something without a name be real? Yet, they know it is real. They live with it every day. It becomes so much easier to only talk to those people who believe you.

# The Goodsons

Richard Goodson won't deny how frustrating Sarah's illness is for him and their family. "He admitted that he thought I was just lazy and liked to sleep . . . if he can't see it then it doesn't exist." Over time, Richard came to accept her illness, though they still don't discuss it openly with friends, neighbors, and extended family. Not even all of the children are aware of the extent of her chronic fatigue and how stressors like their poor decisions influence their mother's physical health.

Aaron, who still lives at home, understands her illness better than the older children. He is aware of how her fatigue episodes require him to do more chores and take on more responsibility, but he doesn't talk about it. That's just how things are; there is no point in bringing other people into it.

# The Clowards

When Jessica was first diagnosed with fibromyalgia, she was very sensitive to light; however, her sensitivity has decreased over time. During the initial diagnosis period, when Jessica showed symptoms of suicidal depression, Justin duct taped black trash bags on the outside of the windows so the light wouldn't bother her. Everyone could see that, but the Clowards still had trouble convincing others Jessica's situation was real.

Their own daughter, a doctor, believed fibromyalgia was a hoax, a phony diagnosis. Even though her own mother was now diagnosed with the illness, it took years of conversations to convince her it was real. As the trash bags were removed from the Clowards' windows, Jessica became very involved with the fibromyalgia support community. Doing so opened her eyes to the number of people suffering with ailments she thought she and her family had faced alone.

# The Swintons

The diagnosis of Kari's multiple sclerosis is only a few years old and still easy to deny. She is more open with friends and family than most; they all know it's there. They watch the deterioration of her abilities to work effectively, serve others, and emotionally invest in challenging relationships with an alcoholic husband and distant children. They want to help. She would rather do it on her own. She's fine, so stop fussing.

Adam owns a motorcycle and expressed concerns over Kari riding it. She enjoys doing so, though Adam is worried her imbalance will get her into a life-threatening accident if she continues to ride it. Kari understands his discomfort but doesn't want to hear his concerns. She appreciates her mother's desire to help out, but Kari believes she can do it on her own. She "didn't want to accept it was a real physical problem" and feels it is her responsibility to protect others from the pain and fear her illness causes.

# The Franklins

Jennifer had heard of fibromyalgia before her own diagnosis, and she believed it was a lazy person's disease. She now understands that it's real and explains it this way: "Very seldom do people know how much pain I'm in." Her diagnosis and divorce from a man who was both mentally and verbally abusive were happening at the same time. Her illness made it impossible for her to work to support her family, yet she was unable to receive unemployment compensation because fibromyalgia was not yet a widely accepted diagnosis. Her teenage daughter took on the role of mother and provider, growing up much more quickly than any teenager should have to.

Nobody understood what Jennifer and her family were going through. Nobody could help. During that time, she hunkered down with her daughters and did everything she could to make sure they were alright. Her daughters did the same for her.

# Other "Families"

Every teen in the wilderness program Taralyn worked for had to learn how to make bow drill fires in order to progress through the program. Every teen was initially so absorbed by his or her own anger and discomfort in the new situation that he or she didn't allow anyone else in. "That's nice you've made over 100 fires with your bow drill. You can't possibly understand how hard this is for me, just leave me alone." Little did they realize just how well everyone in their group did understand exactly what they were experiencing. They had all been there. They all knew what it was like to be dumped in the middle of nowhere with people you didn't know and couldn't trust. They all knew the feeling of desperation to get that first fire, because you know it's your only ticket back home to civilization where things are familiar and make sense. They all hated watching new students struggle for weeks and sometimes months to get their first fire when they had the tools to help them succeed. They had all learned to be patient. Eventually, struggling students would turn to other students or staff for help and get their fires. And they would all wonder the same thing: "Why didn't I ask for help earlier?"

Many of the children Taralyn worked with in orphanages were severely handicapped in one way or another. Many of the single parent families we know have either a parent or child with some form of chronic illness or disability. Many of the family stories in this book include a divorce. It is important to recognize you are not alone. People have walked the path you are on. We've yet to encounter a family who doesn't go through some period of denial and withdrawal, and some situations are certainly easier to hide than others. Admittedly, it seems easier to hide than to face reality and ask for help. We ache for those who are hiding and know from experience that in closing your doors to others, you are opening your doors to demons by pretending you can fight your battles alone.

# CHAPTER 4

# Battling Demons

Riding a raft through rapids is not a leisurely activity. You don't even sit normally. Instead, you straddle the side of the raft as if you're riding a horse and clamp your thigh muscles tightly so you don't fall out as you paddle. It is easy to settle into a routine and get cocky, but that's dangerous. That's when someone relaxes and falls into the raging torrent, which is exactly what one of our teenage male companions did. He got comfortable with the routine, relaxed, fell into the rushing river, and started screaming like a little girl. We had been told what to do if we fell in: relax, lie back onto your life vest, and let the river carry you. That is not what he did. He panicked. He started thrashing about, trying to fight the river. He completely gave in to the demon of fear and unbridled emotion. Consequently, the river threatened to consume him.

Our family quickly learned fear and unbridled emotion could be devastating. Battling these demons became almost more difficult than battling the disease itself. Teresa started out filled with compassion and hope for Stuart, but as weeks gave way to months and months gave way to years, it was hard to maintain these positive feelings. Taralyn adopted a constant worry of how much longer she would have with her daddy before the good Lord took him home. Living away from her parents and siblings made it easy to just not talk about it. By insisting to the outside world that everything was normal, we blocked everyone from realizing we needed help and support. You can't see pain. You can't see fatigue. The only thing outsiders can see are the activities that aren't happening.

The yard fell into disrepair, Teresa and Stuart became uninvolved in community events and melted into the woodwork; they then felt neglected and ignored when no one offered solace. They were worried about the opinions of others but did nothing to create positive opinions. Uninformed comments caused pain. Taralyn felt alone when her friends didn't "ask the right questions." Rather than talking about what she was feeling and dealing with in her life, she sat back and waited for someone to figure out something was wrong, even though she was smiling and saying she was okay. Ironically, we were the biggest demons in our story as we shut the blinds and kept the details to ourselves.

"This isn't Stuart talking, it's the pain talking. This isn't Stuart's behavior, it's medication induced. I am not going to react to that which is not intended." This mantra would swirl through Teresa's head over and over again. Make no mistake: a good attitude may not change the situation, but it can certainly make it easier to bear. Every time Teresa would give in to the temptation to keep score, fight back, or rage against the hopelessness of it all, the situation would deteriorate. Bitterness breeds despair, anger, and resentment. A home filled with such emotions is not a safe place. In such a home, everyone is at risk of failure.

For every demon the chronically ill face, there is a corollary demon for the family. For Stuart, the struggles are pretty straightforward. Who wouldn't swing between despair, melancholy, frustration, resentment, worthlessness, and rage?

"The polyps are back."

Stuart's last "successful" sinus surgery had taken place only three weeks ago.

"To tell you the honest truth, Teresa, I'm stumped. I don't know what to do other than go in and get them out again."

The words oozed over Teresa like molten lead. Every surgery removed offending tissue, but it also removed memory, joy, and hope. Each setback became one more cross for her to bear. Each season of recovery added to the growing list of what would not be accomplished at home.

The medical world responds to pain by throwing medication at it. Once you get ahead of the pain with the right amount of medication, you should stay ahead of the pain by maintaining that level of medication. It can be a very effective fix when dealing with short-term pain. As the pain levels lessen, the need for medication lessens. But it's not so simple with chronic illness: unrelenting pain typically stays around.

Following the standard routine, doctors tried to throw medication at Stuart's pain until Stuart was ahead of it. Therein lay the danger; they asked him to make a long-term commitment. Medication may be beneficial in the short term, but can be habit-forming and create dependency in the long term. As the body adapts to medication, more and more is needed to maintain efficacy. Medical professionals may be quite confident there is no chance of dependency or side effects during withdrawal because medical literature does not address using the medication long term. Consequently, they may be just as surprised as the patient when withdrawal is catastrophic.

Time and again well-intentioned physicians would lure Stuart into this vicious cycle. Eventually, due to personal research and recognizing unsubstantiated complications from long-term use, we decided it was time to discontinue a medication. Stuart is not an addict. There has never been any recreational abuse of his medications, but we know what detoxification and withdrawal look like because we have witnessed it numerous times. Even caring medical professionals may throw up their hands in despair at this point. They are walking uncharted territory because the literature says the drug is not addictive; the literature suggests there will not be complications or withdrawal symptoms. In our experience, the literature is often wrong.

Stuart found ways to self-medicate through the pain by altering his patterns. Less movement equaled less pain. He became sedentary. But just being idle wasn't enough; something needed to distract him from the pain. He found that as long as there was something to capture his attention, the pain lessened. But it couldn't be something that required too much thought. In essence, the activity needed to be pretty mindless. Television, surfing the Internet, participating in news-based chat rooms, and reading newspapers and fantasy literature met Stuart's needs. Of course, this means Stuart was and still is frequently behind a screen or printed page. It is often easier for him to not have to think through the pain to participate in conversations. Hiding in plain sight became a habit.

Stuart became completely self-aware as his medical complications magnified. He could predict with perfect accuracy when a sinus infection was around the corner, when a gout flare-up would occur, when an ulcer was bleeding, when a joint was degrading, when an abscess was growing, when something was seriously wrong. Frequent self-diagnostics throughout the day averted severe complications and led to preventive care earlier, but it also consumed conversations and much of Teresa's attention.

Stuart's self-induced pain management became an entry point for some of the demons Teresa battled. She found it hard to feel engaged with the back of Stuart's head. She became frustrated when she had to repeat conversations because the distractions kept her from being fully heard. It's hard not to feel marginalized when the main topic of conversation is always someone else. Teresa learned not to look to Stuart for sympathy or care, not because he didn't feel love or concern, but because she knew he couldn't handle one more issue on his plate. Anger and resentment easily slip into such situations, with the potential to cause huge rifts in a family—in our family.

Taralyn has watched Stuart and Teresa's relationship throughout the course of her father's illness and learned much from doing so. Her pet demons of all-consuming concern for others and feelings of helplessness extend to both Stuart and Teresa. The unadulterated truth be told, she worries more about Teresa. Stuart still faces demons every day, but they are old enemies. He knows how to cage them. Although he will occasionally set them free, it's never long before they are back in the cage. Teresa, on the other hand, faces new battles every day. Every success and failure, every pain and sorrow, every moment of change has the potential to become a challenging new emotional demon in light of Stuart's illness.

First, Stuart received a dramatic cut in pay with the promise of more to come, leading him to look elsewhere for employment. Stuart's new work schedule of working seven days then having seven days off dramatically altered our family dynamic. His new income was even less than his postcut pay was. Teresa went to work part-time to help make up the difference in pay and give Stuart the courage needed to make the change. Stuart attended important life events that fell during an off week but usually missed those that fell during a work week. His workday started in the predawn hours, resulting in a huge shift in when he went to bed. Teenage children were expected to be quiet by 8:00 p.m. because Dad was sleeping right behind the living room wall.

Teresa worked part-time for nearly two years, but the benefit of extra income was overshadowed by the needs of family at home. We strongly believe a mother's key role is to nurture the family. Creating responsible law-abiding citizens, meeting spiritual and physical needs, and teaching family members to love and serve one another is a fulltime job. As Stuart's needs multiplied,

Teresa's absence was putting the family at risk of failure. When Teresa's boss suggested her children could raise themselves, she realized the only person who would make those kids a priority was she. Teresa came home.

It wasn't long before Stuart came to believe he needed to change his work schedule again. He felt like the swing shift would be a better fit for him. The early-morning shift was grueling for him to balance with a house full of teenagers who stayed up late, so his schedule switched again. His new shift went from 1:00 p.m. to 11:00 p.m. He may have been happier with this schedule, but the rest of us hated it. Important life events that occurred during his work week would be missed. For the kids, it was as if Dad was gone every other week. They wouldn't see him for days at a time. Family rituals of scripture reading and prayer were dramatically challenged. Yet on his off weeks, Stuart was completely present, with no distractions from work left undone or a lack of sleep. He was there for everything. Still, if Teresa and the kids had been given the choice, they would have returned Stuart to the day shift, even though something compelled Stuart to insist this schedule was best.

Schedules continued to shift as medical conditions magnified. Due to seemingly countless surgeries and illnesses, off weeks became filled with two to three doctor visits a week, countless scheduled procedures, and runs to the pharmacy. Over twenty hours a week were filled with such activities. It was time to adapt again.

Demons are relentless during such times of constant change, and each time a demon reared its ugly head, our family was presented with a choice: we could embrace the trial and give in to it, allowing ourselves to be consumed by the fire of resentment and loss, or we could choose to rise above it. Trust us, we know this is not easy, and we didn't always take the high road. We still wage this war on a daily basis, though we've learned more ways to win over the years. It sounds so simple on paper, but the reality of facing these demons is like climbing Mount Everest.

The biggest lesson Teresa learned in the midst of battling the demons of Stuart's chronic illness could be reduced to a simple phrase we've already used: "Don't keep score." It sounds trite, but we can't emphasize the depth of power found in keeping this rule. Every time Teresa allowed herself to add to the "unfair list" and wallow in little hurts and trials, they magnified a hundredfold. When Teresa let the lists of all she did, all she sacrificed, and all the ways she served Stuart stack up in her head, they became destructive distractions. If her energy was focused on compiling lists, she ceased to be authentic in her service. It all became just one more notch to add to the scorecard, one more burden to bear. The resulting weight of those burdens increased the longing for a return to normal, a normal that would never return. The magnification of burdens tempted her to allow trials to define her and her family. When the focus became the crucible itself, the trial had the power to make her bitter, whereas focusing on the joys of life in spite of the winds swirling around her continues to make her better and stronger. Focusing on the joys continues to make our family stronger.

# The Tidlunds

The moment Tiffany and Bryan heard the words "Hadley has a tumor," demons opened fire. Thoughts of cancer treatments and loss of life immediately took force. They were scared and felt incredibly alone. Their two little girls would need to be cared for, and no family could come to help. Who among strangers would care for two little girls who were also scared and confused? How would they ever afford surgeries and treatments? How could they face the loss of a child? Cancer was killing Tiffany's grandma, and her mind immediately turned to loved ones lost and about to be lost. How could she bear the deaths of both a grandma and a daughter? She couldn't; there was no way she would make it through such a terrible turn of events.

Worst-case scenarios swirled through her head as she fell into her husband's arms, unable to hold the tears back. She sobbed, unable to offer Bryan much comfort as the same scenarios washed over him. Headaches never scared her before, but now she felt as if the fear, loneliness, and despair would never leave her. Every headache became a death sentence in her mind as she and her husband left their two babies with strangers and took their daughter to the hospital where more strangers would perform emergency brain surgery. In that moment, they could not feel the angels surrounding them.

# The Crandalls

"If I don't get some time alone, I'm going to go insane!"

Julie said it again and again. It seemed to her that no one was hearing her. Marcus missed her and Kassie desperately. When they were actually home at the same time, Marcus wanted to express that love and longing in physical ways, but Julie was exhausted. The last thing she wanted or needed was physical contact. She wanted sleep. She wanted space. She wanted to remember what it was like to be a young mother who made cupcakes and took her little girl to the park. All she did anymore was study treatments and side effects and hold her daughter's frail little hand during spinal taps and more. No one ever considered her needs or her sorrow. All she ever did was answer questions about Kassie and try to hold Marcus at bay. Sure, she knew this wasn't the way to nurture a marriage, but was it so bad if Marcus had to work long hours and sacrifice his wants too? When Kassie got better they could fix everything else. Until then, too bad.

Marcus was desperately alone. He was sure Julie hadn't intended it to be this way, but somehow a huge chasm had formed between them. It felt to him like his only purpose was to bring home a paycheck and pay the bills. No one asked him if he was scared or lonely. He was just supposed to man up and work. He felt completely cut off from Kassie and her treatments. Weeks would pass between the times he would see her awake. He was becoming a stranger to his daughter, and his wife didn't want anything to do with him. This was no way to live. He felt so cut off from everything, and now he was cut off from his extended family again, too. Julie didn't want any outsiders in their home. Marcus had become an outsider. All he could do was to not give up. He needed help. Their family needed help.

# The Kellers

"I didn't choose this. I don't even know who I'm married to anymore."

Shayna Keller struggles as she watches her husband transform into someone she doesn't even know. Her once optimistic husband is now prone to serious depression and reaches a point where he physically can't help anymore. If there are too many stimuli in the evenings, he just shuts down and disappears, sometimes going to bed as early as 7:00 p.m.

With nine children in the Keller home, there are often too many stimuli. The children are hurt when their father disappears or snaps at them, and they have a hard time understanding what they did wrong. They did nothing wrong; Sam just gets frustrated with his limited abilities and constant pain and takes it out on whoever adds the last straw to his pile. The explanation of why he snaps rarely takes away the pain, though. Family traditions and routines are gone, and the family is sometimes angry and resentful about that. His boys miss wrestling with him more than anything. His daughters miss their dad's personalized teasing attention. Sam just feels guilty and helpless all the time.

"Why me? Wouldn't I be much more helpful in the kingdom of God if I was healthy? Wouldn't I be much more help to my family if I were healthy?" The pain, medicinal side effects, inability to get up early or stay up late, and worry wear on him and the whole family. Both he and Shayna have gained weight and feel helpless to change it. Shayna's parents have expressed concern about her physical appearance: the weight gain, how often she wears sweats, the hair left disheveled. Shayna just doesn't have time. The Kellers are on the "edge of the cliff," doing their best to keep from falling, often unable to see the hands holding them up.

# The Zales

Lorena and Matthew Zale laugh when you ask them what their friends would say about the family. "What friends?" Lorena's illness is so overwhelming that previously cherished friendships have fallen by the wayside. Lorena can't leave her home, and Matthew is so exhausted after caring for Lorena and their son that he has no energy for others. At least, that's what he would tell you.

Matthew misses doing previously enjoyed joint activities with Lorena. They used to play ice hockey and go camping and biking together, but those days are gone. This loss of vitality is hard for Lorena, too. She has gained weight and continually battles depression. Matthew fears their son resents Lorena's illness, and both have noticed he spends less time with her. In fact, the family rarely spends time all together anymore. More often than not, time is spent in pairs. Matthew spends time with their son or with Lorena but rarely with both together. He doesn't realize what an angel he is to both of them.

# The Goodsons

Richard is up and running in the morning "before I'm even alive," says Sarah. She laughs good-naturedly when saying this, but you can see the pain in her eyes. She aches to be able to care for him, her children, and their home as she used to. She can't even be physically intimate with her husband without consequences for days afterward. Such activities have to be scheduled when she knows she'll have at least a few days to stay in bed and recover afterward. Guilt and sadness wash over her when she has to look her little boy in the face and tell him she can't play or help him with something because she's just too tired. "I get depressed that my husband [and son are] having to do all the work . . . I want to be me again," Sarah expresses.

Richard has noticed a cycle; Sarah will eat more when she is depressed, gain weight, and then feel depressed because of her weight gain. She tries hard to control what she eats but can't exercise to stay fit. This battle seems unrelenting. It is frustrating for her family to watch her suffer helplessly. They wish they could do more but know they can't.

# The Clowards

Jessica has learned ways to control her severe depression but still carries sadness around with her constantly. She sees clearly how her illness has affected her family. In particular, she's noticed that her children seem to keep a guard up around her now, almost as if they can't trust her anymore. It's the illness they can't trust. The effects of the illness often make Jessica somewhat unpredictable. Will it be a good day or a bad day? She can't handle relationships and traditions with extended family at all anymore because it's too challenging. It hurts too much, and she has less to give to her immediate family. Caring about traditions is hard because they take so much of her energy. And most of her energy is expended in reaching out to others in similar situations. This keeps her busy and distracted, but Justin misses her. The kids miss her. Still, they support her efforts to be a stronghold for others.

# The Swintons

Kari Swinton's illness is too much for Adam; he just can't handle watching her suffer. Alcohol is the only thing that deadens the pain, yet the deadening of his pain created a massive rift in their relationship. Thinking the alcohol may help her too, Adam took Kari out drinking one night. It deadened her physical pain, but her children and her mother were furious. Adam's efforts to help only drove the wedge deeper. Kari had to think about her health and her children. She didn't want a second failed marriage, but the stress of watching Adam go out drinking every night with friends and seemingly never helping around the house or with the family became too much to bear.

The couple is now divorced. As Kari's illness progresses, her symptoms worsen. Her children now leave reminders posted on her bathroom mirror about conversations they had because they know she won't remember later. The family spends less time together than ever, and Kari doesn't know how to change that. She knows it needs to change. She is beginning to allow people to help.

# The Franklins

If you ask Jennifer about her pain, she will candidly express, "I hate it." No sugarcoating. Her illness tore her life—her family's life—to pieces. She blames her illness for her divorce, the loss of her job, her financial troubles, and her pain and fatigue. She constantly battles frustration and confusion. She often feels lazy but incapable of making changes.

Each day brings new challenges, and Jennifer never makes plans anymore; she's tired of letting people down. She has suffered from memory loss and attributes this in part to her pain medications. She tries to take as little pain medication as possible, though this contributes to a more sedentary lifestyle than she prefers.

Her youngest daughter, now in her thirties, is single and cares for her mother. When Jennifer lost her job, they lived on her daughter's student loans until Jennifer was able to receive financial support in other ways. She still expresses guilt and shame at having to depend so wholly on a daughter she used to support.

# Other "Families"

A wave of guilt washed over Taralyn as she left little Austin behind at that orphanage. How many other people had walked away from him in his short life? Now she was just another disappointment, another person he had finally trusted only to be abandoned again. Taralyn wondered how quickly her own heart would heal this time. It had been five years since she'd left the children at the boarding school, and she still ached for them at times. After spending four months loving them, teaching them, and singing them lullabies as she tucked them in at night, she was gone. Just gone. Looking at pictures and reading journal entries about time spent with those little ones feels like looking at pictures and reading journal entries about loved ones who have passed away. Taralyn will never see those children again, and they will never see her again. The worst part is how frequently this scene is replayed in their lives.

"I can't do it. I'm not going to survive this program. I can't hike." Every teen in wilderness therapy went through this phase. It looked different on each person, though. Some would pretend to faint. After all, if you fainted, you got a break from hiking. Others would fall onto the ground screaming and kicking as if they were two years old. Still, others would sit down where they were and quietly refuse to move. The staff's job was to safely get the group moving again while staving off the anger other group members felt about being inconvenienced by the new kid's stubborn unwillingness to be a team player. "I was never that bad when I was new."

Mother Nature is unpredictable, and her lessons are never the same. One thing is for certain: She will teach you, like it or not. Anger, frustration, confusion, sadness, loneliness, mistrust, and fear were constantly present amongst groups of at-risk teens and the staff who worked with them. It only took one person to rise above it.

All families face their share of demons. Trials such as chronic illness, death, addiction, and divorce relish in the company of individually tailored demons designed to destroy families. You will face them. That's a fact. Although it's hard to remember, it is also a fact that you never have to fight your battles alone. Real-life angels surround us all; we just need to learn where to find them and how to see them.

CHAPTER 5

# Real-Life Angels

"Help me, help me, help me!"

We've never been sure if Taralyn acted out of a desire to genuinely help or out of a desire to make the irritating screaming stop. She simply leaned over the edge of the raft, grabbed the boy's life vest, pulled the boy onboard, deposited him facedown in the middle of the raft, then returned to paddling for our lives. It was quite the moment. The boy was humiliated but overcome with gratitude. Taralyn was pretty proud of herself. Teresa couldn't stop laughing. We need to confess that we were pretty impressed with ourselves when we reached the landing safely. Talk about a sense of accomplishment! We had not only fulfilled a long-held mutual goal; we had personally fought valiantly to make it successful. Our self-absorbed pride bloated when the river guide clasped our arms and declared, "Thank you! We never would have made it without you."

That's when reality struck. We were humbled instantly. The truth is, for all our rowing, we never would have survived without the river guide. She knew the river, she knew how to steer, and she stayed constant and focused. She was the real angel of this trip. Just as she served as our angel that day, angels have surrounded us individually and as a family in Stuart's battle with chronic illness.

Taralyn was blessed to live with Grandma Clark, Stuart's mother, during the final nine months of Grandma Clark's life. They shared a birthday and had always been close, but those months together brought them closer than ever.

Grandma's list of ailments was impressive, culminating in endometrial cancer that later metastasized to her lungs and brain. But she rarely complained. Scores of people dropped by the house in her final weeks to see her one last time. It was as if they were coming to Mecca to be blessed by Grandma before she passed. And every one of them would tell you they were her favorite. She listened to and cared about every individual who walked through her unlocked door, young or old, no matter his or her story. Under her grandma's tutelage, Taralyn increased in patience, wisdom, and understanding.

Although Grandma had enough love for everybody, her fiercest love was reserved for her children. She was Teresa's respite. Teresa knew Grandma listened. She would often call and talk to Grandma for hours about Stuart's health and her own wellbeing. Teresa opened up to Grandma more than she did to others, and Grandma responded with love and patience. The conversation always ended with Grandma expressing gratitude to Teresa for caring so wholly for her son.

Teresa felt an incredible amount of support from Grandma and often expressed gratitude for her angelic mother-in-law who simply appreciated all that Teresa was doing. Taralyn feels that same gratitude to Teresa for caring so wholly for her daddy. Caregivers are angels, though often unnoticed. They sacrifice their time, leisure pursuits, and often their own health in love and service to the one they care for. Grandma's dearest friends constantly thanked Taralyn for living with her near the end: "You just don't know what a relief it is to have someone there during the nights." Taralyn would tell you she gained far more from living with Grandma than she ever gave. Those nine months, although a challenge, are months she would never give back. They have helped mold her into who she is today. Teresa will tell you a similar story. Although living with a husband battling chronic illness is never easy, she is blessed by her service to him. He couldn't make it without her, nor could she make it without him.

Like Grandma, individuals battling intense trials often serve as angels to others. There are some things that didn't change after Stuart's troubles began. Before he and Teresa married, Stuart had determined that he would declare his love for her and share a laugh with her every day. This tradition continued in spite of the swirling mists of change. The source of the humor altered (much of it was now health based), but still it endured. He continued to joke and tease the kids, serving as an angel to the whole family by releasing some of the tension his illness created. Taralyn, ever a Daddy's girl, continues to feel loved and supported as Stuart makes sacrifices, in spite of his burdens, to spend time with her. Learning to recognize our real-life angels through Stuart's illness has altered our perceptions dramatically. Real-life angels surround us. Sometimes they come in the form of a stranger opening a door, a neighbor dropping by with a treat, or a loved one giving support through an unexpected phone call.

Total strangers stand ready to become angels. We learned that best the first time we hauled Stuart off to the woods in a wheelchair. We were pushing him around a favored geyser basin trail. Overall, it was pretty flat and easy, but the best part of the trail was accessed via a steep grade. Taralyn, Taunalee, and Teresa were able to provide the drag necessary for Stuart to get down the hill, but coming back up was nearly impossible. First, Taunalee pushed until she got too tired. Then Teresa stepped in for a push until she got too tired. Taralyn was determined to finish the job. She took a running lunge at the wheelchair and started jogging up that hill with all her might, but her might wasn't quite enough. About halfway up the hill, her progress slowed to a halt as the chair veered to the left and threatened to tip over. Taralyn was out of steam, the rest of us were still at the bottom of the hill, and the handle wraps started to pull off in the strain. As Taralyn turned to glance back downhill, a Frenchman appeared out of nowhere. "Do you need help?" Without even waiting for a reply, he wrapped his hands around the wheelchair handles, leaned his entire frame into the chair, and got Stuart to the top of the hill in one smooth glide. Taralyn called, "Thank you!" as he walked away, and Teresa and Taunalee made it to the top of the hill. We had never pictured an angel with a French accent and European fashion sense. Yet on that day, that is exactly what our angel looked like. As suddenly as he had appeared, he was gone.

By the time Grandma reached her deathbed, Taralyn had spent nine months facing trying circumstances with her. They had been through surgeries, radiation treatment, infections, pneumonia, falls, and the first year of Taralyn's graduate studies together. Taralyn knew Grandma would go that day. She just knew it. Oddly, that knowledge strengthened her. She was ready to see Grandma released from her suffering and didn't understand the uncontrollable sobs escaping from her aunt each time there was a pause in Grandma's breathing. Her parents and sister were on their way to Grandma's house, and she was happy she wouldn't be alone that night. Not that she was actually alone; her aunt and two uncles were there with her, but she didn't feel particularly close to any of them. She loved them, but growing up far away from them had prevented the formation of strong bonds. She feels differently now.

Taralyn sat next to her uncle as Grandma drew her last breath and immediately felt as if she were outside of her own body, watching herself fall to pieces. Uncontrollable sobs racked her body until her uncle took her in his arms. Then she could feel again. She leaned against him as her aunt wrapped her arms around them both and another uncle offered a sweet prayer of gratitude for a life well lived, and Taralyn began to heal. It was just a simple touch and a simple prayer, but her uncles and aunt saved her that night. For Taralyn, living away from family and home, a hug almost always comes from an angel.

After Grandma's passing, Taralyn's worries about Stuart became a heavier burden to bear. She wasn't ready to say goodbye to him either. Her thesis research could not have begun at a better time. As she spent time with families facing similar trials, her eyes were opened to the infinite number of people who face hard things in life. As she shared with them the reasons she was interested in studying families with a parent battling chronic illness, they became her angels. They had opened their doors and hearts to a complete stranger, laying it all on the line. Taralyn spent hours in each of their homes, observing family routines and asking hard questions, and she came away feeling strengthened. As she listened to them, they listened to her, and that small act of kindness made them angels. As she told friends and colleagues about her thesis research, they also began to share their stories.

Marjorie Horan was dying. Her son Jonathan and his father Don knew it. It was difficult for them to bear, but Marjorie remained a strength and blessing to her family and others until her dying day. One evening, she lay on the couch, unable to physically help with dinner. Don, who had rarely cooked a meal in his life, was taking on the role of family cook. Back and forth he would go, between the couch Marjorie was lying on and the kitchen. Step by step she told him what to do, and he did it. In the midst of this, a friend dropped by. She was also battling illness and didn't know how she would make dinner for her family that night. She didn't have the strength. Marjorie listened and then gave Don one final instruction to complete their meal. Marjorie's friend left that evening with their meal, boxed up and still warm. Jonathan doesn't remember what they ate that night, but it doesn't matter. He remembers his angel mother acting in loving kindness until the end.

Stuart and Teresa live in a different state than their grandchildren and most of their children. When the children were young, reunions were held biannually with Teresa's side of the family. Our extended family grew up knowing and loving each other because we all made sacrifices to be able to spend time together. It wasn't long after Taunalee, the baby, moved away to college before Teresa and Stuart began family reunions of their own. At least once a year our family gathers, all of us, and spends time laughing and playing together. Tiffany and Steven and each of their spouses don't realize they are angels. Stuart needs to hold and tease his grandchildren, and Teresa needs to feel physical love and support from her children. Each time one of the kids makes an effort to be with Teresa and Stuart, he or she serves as an angel.

Real-life angels have come to our family in all forms, often years before we knew we needed them. They sometimes even felt like destroying angels when we first met. Teresa and Taralyn were both serving as leaders at an annual weeklong girls camp for their church. Everyone in camp feared Susie. She was the first to mock any little mistake. Cross her mood and you were sure to be blasted with a tirade of foul and angry words. Yet, there was something about her walk that begged attention. She walked like she was in pain. Out of nowhere the thought came to Teresa: "Offer to wash her feet." Teresa's mind screamed out in resistance, "Wash her feet, are you kidding me? I'd just as soon wash out her mouth; besides, she'd never let me." Again the thought returned, more forcefully, "Offer to wash her feet, *now*." So, she did. "Susie, you look like you're in pain. Can I wash your feet?"

Teresa thought Susie would turn her down cold, but she didn't. Shock washed over her face, but there was also a hint of relief as she accepted the offer. While Taralyn grabbed a basin of warm water, Teresa led Susie to a bench and began removing her shoes. What she found shocked her to the core; Susie wasn't wearing socks and her feet were covered with broken and bleeding blisters. Well into the third day of camp, she had hiked miles on those mistreated feet. When asked where her socks were she confessed she didn't have any. She had been too embarrassed to let anyone know. When we slipped her feet into the basin of warm water, tears pooled at the corners of Susie's eyes. Concerned we were hurting her, we started to pull her feet back out until she declared, "Teresa, this is the nicest thing anyone has ever done for me. It feels like a never-ending hug."

As the warm water enveloped Susie's feet, a wave of pure love for her enveloped our hearts. We no longer saw a cold and bitter young woman; we saw a damaged child in desperate need of attention. The transition was contagious. We had started washing her feet in camp when none of the other youth were around, but before we were finished several of the other teen campers returned. When they saw Susie's feet they ran to their tents and brought out extra socks and first aid supplies to get her through the rest of the week. Without anyone being assigned, everyone in camp took on the care of Susie's feet. Susie's surliness gave way to gratitude. As others served her, they helped to heal her wounded heart.

One could argue that we were the angels that day, but that is simply not the case. Susie's need for service was a tremendous gift. We not only discovered the power found in a simple act of kindness but we also came to understand the power service holds for opening and healing our hearts. In learning that lesson, we were prepared for a future need. Foot rubs lessen the pain of the afflicted, but they also heal the heart of the caregiver. Teresa has implemented this gift into the care of Stuart. When her demons swirl, the greatest tool in her arsenal is to rub Stuart's feet.

# The Tidlunds

If you ask Tiffany and Bryan about their experiences surrounding Hadley's tumor, you will almost certainly hear two stories. They had moved just before Hadley's diagnosis and knew very few people in their community. Yet in their time of need, the community rallied in their support. The Tidlunds came home from the hospital almost a week after Hadley's surgery to a clean house, well-cared-for children, and an army of new friends. Hundreds of people had been offering prayers for their family, and they felt those prayers. One of their greatest worries was how their daughter's $70,000 emergency brain surgery would be paid for. They certainly couldn't afford it; that sum was more than Bryan's annual salary. In discussing this concern with the hospital, the hospital determined they qualified for financial assistance and covered the entire bill. Even institutions can serve as angels.

# The Crandalls

"I'm here for two weeks. That was the least expensive airfare, so I had to take it."

Julie and Marcus both looked shell-shocked at Tonia's news. Tonia's willingness to stay in the hospital for the week of Kassie's chemotherapy treatment was heaven-sent, but what would they do with her for the next week? She'd left her own young family to be there for them and had made a substantial fiscal sacrifice to fly to their aid. They couldn't kick her out into a hotel. They'd have to cope with her visit.

"Kassie's getting better, you know. It's time you start being a couple again." In their hearts, they knew Tonia was right. But the shattered schedules and awkward silences had become a huge part of their lives; it was as if they had never lived any other way. Tonia would not be ignored. She also didn't insist on being involved in whatever they did. On the contrary, she was determined to spend as little time with them as possible. Every night she spent in their home she sent them out for a drive, a date, or dinner, all without Kassie. While Tonia played with and cared for Kassie, her parents tried to reconnect. Tonia's choice had annoyed them at first, but the time they spent alone each evening reminded them of what they had been missing.

While Marcus worked during the days, Tonia would ask Julie what she and Kassie had done for fun before Kassie became ill. She would then insist they do it again. Sugar cookies, walks in the park, and snuggling up to watch a movie began to supersede regimented nap times. For the first time in months, the entire family began to feel joy. Tonia had become a real-life angel to them. They were truly sorry to see her leave, but Tonia's visit had also given them a vision of what future visits could look like. They found the courage to instruct other visitors to help by modeling Tonia's actions.

# The Kellers

Shayna Keller doesn't see herself as an angel, but Sam sees her that way. She is ashamed when her compassion wears thin, but Sam often notes, "She does it all. I'm so appreciative to Shayna." She really does do it all. Her days are spent caring for their nine children, listening to their stories, taxiing them to concerts and plays and recitals, and teaching them to be responsible and caring adults. She also takes care of Sam. She listens to him, helps him with his health regimen, and tries to keep the kids quiet enough that they won't increase his pain or cause him to snap. She does her best to ensure the family continues to spend time together doing fun activities. She is an angel.

It took some time for Sam's employer to understand and accept the reality of Sam's illness. Through seeking to understand Sam's situation and allowing Sam to keep his job, Sam's employer became an angel. Sam visited a therapist during one stage of his illness and was relieved to be able to talk to somebody, to have somewhere to unload his thoughts and emotions. That therapist was just doing his job, but he was also an angel. Every member of Sam's strong support system is a much-needed help to Sam and his family. And Sam, by making sacrifices to continue to support his family in spite of the illness threatening to consume him, is an angel to them.

# The Zales

Lorena knows what angels she has in her life. Matthew gives everything he has to care for her and raise their son. In spite of the hardships, he remains by her side. She knows he will never leave her, and that knowledge brings her peace. Her father is the other angel in her life. Though she didn't have a particularly close relationship with him before, she does now. He takes her to doctor appointments, helps around the house, and often calls to see how she's doing. Lorena's dad and Matthew even built a screen room on the side of the house so she can spend time outside on nice days.

Matthew and Lorena are service-oriented people and have given much of their lives in service to others. They now spend most of their time and energy caring for each other, but neither begrudges the situation. It's hard, but people do hard tasks every day. They can too. They also serve outside of their home in ways that are suited for them. Taralyn's thesis research was a perfect opportunity for them: they could help without leaving home. She went to them. Both Matthew and Lorena told her, "I hope it will help." They both hoped talking about their situation would help other families battling similar demons.

# The Goodsons

In spite of Sarah's chronic fatigue, Sarah served as an angel to her mother until her mother's dying day. Her mom could no longer clean her home and didn't have a Richard to take care of things for her. So Sarah took on that role, spending three or four hours a week cleaning and scrubbing her mother's home. She sometimes paid for this with episodes of fatigue, but she was determined to do this service for another.

Richard and Aaron step up and help when Sarah is unable to do so. They do a lot of the cooking and cleaning, and Richard is happy to help because both he and Sarah like a clean, orderly home. This attitude of service is a huge relief to Sarah. Richard has an intense need and desire to do all he can to care for his family, not realizing what an angel he is to Sarah and his children.

# The Clowards

Justin Cloward continues to work a busy job that keeps him away from home much of the time. So as Jessica's troubles stormed on, her daughter stepped into Jessica's shoes. She cared for the house and her mother and prepared meals during that first year of Jessica's severe and all-consuming depression. She still helps. She doesn't think she did anything extraordinary, but Jessica would tell you differently. Her daughter was and still is an angel. In addition to Jessica's daughter, Jessica's therapist was another angel to her. She was able to reach inside Jessica when nobody else could. Some professions overflow with angels.

Jessica has since become active in local and national support communities for those battling chronic illness. She wants to help people through the hard times that are now behind her; she doubtlessly serves as a blessing to countless individuals and families by doing so. Jessica served as an incredible blessing to Taralyn by becoming one of her greatest advocates in finding families to work with during her thesis research. Jessica doesn't offer service to others battling illness alone, though. Her entire family supports her in her efforts to lift and strengthen others.

# The Swintons

The first person Taralyn met in Kari's home was Kari's mother, Donna. Kari opened the door, hurried off to change, and left Taralyn sitting with Donna in the front room. It was obvious Donna loved her daughter. She was often there, especially in the evenings, to help with meals and the kids. She freely provided moral support for Kari as she faced her husband's alcoholism. Kari's friends and coworkers also provided incredible support. It was at their urging she went to the doctor after that initial fall when she lost her balance at a school event. They continue to be a strong and angelic support system for her when family life seems to be falling to pieces. Additionally, Kari is blessed with a strong support network in her extended family. They live close and help often, though her teenage son is often her biggest support. He is attentive and helpful, an angel in Kari's life.

# The Franklins

Whereas most families we have met will tell us stories about their helpers, Jennifer Franklin will specifically mention angels. She knows she never would have made it through her divorce and initial diagnosis of fibromyalgia without the immediate and constant support of her youngest daughter, who has made constant sacrifices to ensure Jennifer's comfort and safety. And although Jennifer's parents have passed away, they continue to be angels for Jennifer. Their memories and stories swirl in her mind and strengthen her in times of despair and loneliness. She is deeply religious and gives credit to the Lord Jesus Christ for her peace during her trials. Her grandkids are "the light of [her] life," and their parents know it. Much effort is put in to make sure Jennifer is able to have loving relationships with those little angels. Much like our own family, the Franklins have pushed Jennifer in a wheelchair through many adventures. Jennifer also has a therapist who has been a huge help to her. Her own grateful attitude is perhaps one of her most powerful blessings: Jennifer is always able to see the silver lining.

# Other "Families"

Taralyn was halfway around the world when Teresa had her heart attack. She received a one-line email: "Mom's had a heart attack and is in the hospital. We'll keep you posted. Love you!" Taralyn had never felt so lost, alone, or helpless. At that time in her life, she was terrible at telling people about the hard circumstances in her life. Truth be told, she still battles the desire to keep those things hidden and protected from others. Her mom's heart attack was no different. She felt like she was going to explode; she just needed to go for a walk to clear her head.

While walking around the campus of the boarding school where she taught, Taralyn ran into one of her favorite students. She smiled and acted happy, but that little boy saw right through her. He took her face in his hands, looked up at her with soft brown eyes and said, "Teachah, yesah happy?" With those broken English words of love and kindness, a wave of peace and calm washed over her. "Yes, I'm happy," she told him. He gave her a tight squeeze and was off, surely unaware of how heaven-sent his actions were that day.

If you ask Taralyn about her experiences volunteering in orphanages and boarding schools or working in day care centers and rehabilitative settings, you won't hear much about the service she rendered. Instead, you will hear all about how much she loves "her babies," how much she misses them, what she learned from them, and how often she prays for them. In each of those different settings, the people Taralyn worked with placed complete trust in her ability to care for them and keep them safe. They had to. Sometimes immediately, but more often eventually, that trust grew into unconditional love. All of the children and teens she has loved and cared for over the years have become her guardian angels as she walks through life. Although she will likely never see them again, memories of them guide and strengthen her as she strives to offer that same unquestioning love and trust to everyone around her.

We hear it all the time: "I really admire your willingness to work with at-risk youth. I could never do that." In truth, the statement gives us pause. It's moments like the one we shared with Susie that led us to hunger for more and dedicate our lives to listening to the stories of others. It's moments like the one we shared with Susie that invite us to become real-life angels ourselves. As we listen to the stories of others, our hearts expand in their behalf. After years of hearing the stories of families at risk, we have come to believe every family is at risk.

By definition, the term "at risk" applies to those who are "vulnerable, especially to abuse or delinquency." We would submit all families from all walks of life are vulnerable. Abuse and delinquency come in countless forms. More often than not they are unintended. The very dynamic of a family sharing their lives and living space invites opportunities for hurt feelings, misunderstanding, misguided intent, neglect, abuse, delinquency, and pain. Conversely, family is also the proving ground for unity, understanding, kindness, sacrifice, sharing, faith, and hope.

In very real ways, family is the ultimate lab for forgiveness and love. Consequently, we declare every family is at risk: they are at risk of failure, but they are also at risk of remarkable success. They are at risk to experience incredibly life-altering trials and uncertainty, but they are also at risk of being blessed and growing through those experiences.

# CHAPTER 6:

# Hidden Blessings

"Never underestimate the healing power of touch . . . Slip in bed beside her and hold her in your arms . . . She needs to feel that physical closeness." Stuart uttered these words to his father-in-law as his mother-in-law lay in critical condition after experiencing a brain aneurism. While everyone was standing stiffly and hesitantly around her still form, Stuart was the one who knew what to do. Years of being on the receiving end of such care had given him the courage and life experience he needed to point out what needed to be done. His compassion and wisdom broke through the fog of the unknown and invited his father-in-law to take a course of action. Stuart's trials had led to hidden blessings. This was not the first time, and it won't be the last.

Looking back on our three worst years, it would be easy to imagine Stuart would lose his job. Twelve surgeries took place, most requiring a full week of recovery and two requiring six weeks of recovery. That's when we came to understand the miracle and blessing of the swing shift. In essence, the swing shift was a divinely directed diversion. None of us had known why Stuart was compelled to be on the swing shift. But now the hidden blessing was evident.

Stuart would push himself to work through a working week then go into surgery or the emergency room on the first morning of his off week. Even if he wasn't fully recovered by the next working week, he could usually get up and going by the start of his 1:00 p.m. shift. In all of that chaos, he only faced two weeks off work without pay or benefits. No other schedule would have survived such a lifestyle.

The seven on, seven off schedule was a miracle for other reasons, too. As the children married and had their own children, the off week allowed Stuart and Teresa to travel and help with new babies, moves, and moments of crisis through three generations of family. He was able to be with his mother through much of her illness. His experiences with illness led him to be compassionate to all who suffer. He can stand in a crowded room and pick out the people in pain. Taralyn and Teresa can do it too. This gift and hidden blessing in Stuart's battle enables us all to reach out more effectively in love and service to others.

Another hidden blessing came as Stuart's father was dying. While Stuart couldn't work due to his ankle injury, his father had lost his ability to communicate. His mother was caring for him alone. Since there were no work responsibilities keeping Stuart in town, we loaded Stuart up in the car and went to join his parents at their home. Just being surrounded by those you love is often the greatest comfort in times of trial. There's also great learning. Carol, Stuart's mother, began tutoring Teresa in what pure love looked like. She never said it in words; she taught through actions.

The way Carol loved and cared for her husband taught Teresa volumes. She laughed over the chaos and expressed gratitude for the time they had together, in spite of it being filled with silence. She was tender and patient and truly found herself through the twenty-four-hour care she provided to her husband.

We lived a dual existence over the following months, traveling between Idaho and Utah as Stuart finally returned to work and his father slowly faded. But the lessons Teresa learned as she watched Carol care for LaMar never faded. Whenever Stuart's situation intensified enough to require constant daily care, it was Carol's example that led Teresa forward.

There are many other hidden blessings resulting from the trying journey Stuart has embarked upon. Episodes of the *Clark Show* still involve laughter, but now they also involve deeper sharing. This shifted after the first time we hauled Stuart off to the forest like a puppy in a kennel. During that trip we plopped him into a camp chair and built up a big campfire. This was new for us because we usually milked every last ounce of daylight for adventure and then ate and played games into the night. This time there was little adventure and a lot more sitting. With the coals banked and Stuart cozy in his chair, we relaxed into a long night of sharing around the campfire.

That night we reminisced about favored memories and adventures, learned all sorts of stories about Stuart as a little boy, and gained an entirely new appreciation for our husband and father. We also realized we could still have great family experiences, even if they were a little less adventurous. We understood that returning to the memories of the past could strengthen us in the present. That night, Stuart remembered much of his youth, and his daughters wanted the rest of the family to experience that too. That night the idea of annual family camping trips was born.

As the kids grew up and built their own families, we had not remained purposeful in our interactions. Deciding to hold an annual campout gave Stuart something to plan and look forward to. It created memory-building events for the grandkids to have with Poppa Stu and Grandma Teresa. Each campout since the first more sedentary adventure has involved an evening of chatting around the fire. As we tell stories about each other and reflect on old memories, our family bond grows ever deeper. While we were always close-knit, we're even closer now.

Since we have had a few close calls when Stuart nearly lost his life, we have come to realize how precious life can be. Thus, we started creating an annual picture book about our time together so the memories stay fresh for everyone, just in case. They contain the shorthand of our lives. Classic quotes. Beauty we witnessed together. And lots of pictures of us enjoying each other and the wonders of our world. All of this has led to an increased openness as to what is really important. We are more quick and comfortable in offering prayers and words of support to one another. We frequently share what we are thankful for. We aren't afraid to ask one another to fast or pray in each other's behalf. We share spiritual thoughts and scripture messages more easily. Everyone makes greater efforts to visit one another. The kids make a conscious effort to come home and help with home projects. Phone calls are made weekly rather than sporadically. Teresa and Stuart have even started a blog for their grandkids. Basically, the hidden blessings of Stuart's illnesses have been remarkable. We never would wish for the trials Stuart (and consequently our family) has been called upon to bear, but we also would never give up the bounteous hidden blessings that have resulted.

# The Tidlunds

The Tidlund's story is rife with hidden blessings. It was hard for Tiffany to call her grandma, who lay on her deathbed, to tell her about Hadley's tumor. Yet, she knew it was important for her to feel involved. Grandma wept as Tiffany told her the diagnosis, and Grandma immediately offered to mail Hadley any stuffed animal she wanted. No child should ever have to experience such problems. Hadley would never see her great-grandma in this life again, and that stuffed panda bear came to represent all of her love and kindness. Although Hadley's tumor has not returned, she still suffers from occasional headaches. In those moments, Grandma's stuffed panda bear is one of the only things that give her comfort. In a very real way, Hadley's tumor and resultant surgery formed an unbreakable bond between Hadley and her great-grandma. Those of us who know and love Hadley's great-grandmother know this will be a blessing to Hadley throughout her life.

The entire Tidlund family is more kind and compassionate towards one another. They try harder to spend time together and listen to each other. Family scripture study has become a priority and continues to bless their lives immeasurably. Partly as a result of Hadley's situation and the difficulty in being far away from family at such a time, Bryan and Tiffany decided to take a substantial pay cut and move closer to family. They are now able to attend important life events and spend time with extended family in meaningful ways. In the shock and pain-filled moment of Hadley's whirlwind diagnosis and surgery, you would not have heard them talk about blessings. But they talk about them now.

# The Crandalls

Marcus and Julie initially struggled to find the hidden blessings in their situation. So many of their plans and dreams had been set aside. So much of what they imagined their lives would be like had been altered. Yet over time, they came to see hidden blessings. In spite of their adamant attempts to push people away, they had developed deeper ties with their extended family. While they still cherished their privacy, they opened their hearts to the benefits of a loving extended family. Julie even felt comfortable enough to visit her in-laws without Marcus from time to time. This proved to be a great boon as Kassie had come to love them deeply during her various treatments. Kassie's illness had healed many rifts in extended family relationships. Her new outgoing nature was also an unanticipated blessing. Prior to the illness, Kassie had been quite shy and clung to her parents. The illness and accompanying kaleidoscope of treatments and caregivers had opened up Kassie's world. She enjoyed visiting her caregivers long after treatments were no longer necessary. She willingly showered grandparents, aunts, uncles, and cousins with kisses when she saw them. She also developed an incredible empathy for anyone who was suffering. She would often pat the hand or scratch the back of someone in need. Her play changed from being bored with her toys to creating elaborate imaginary settings where dolls were ill and required IVs created from yarn and tape. And she kept her mother in stitches and brought laughter back into their home.

At the same time, Marcus discovered he could do hard things, much harder than he had ever imagined. His work ethic and commitment to working in his educational field was deeply magnified. He strived to work smarter, not harder, so he would have more time with home and family. For a season, these hidden blessings enveloped the family and helped them set aside much of the pain and miscommunications of the past.

# The Kellers

The Kellers have always been a close family, but they are closer now. Sam's illness has required the children, particularly the older daughters, to step up and help more around the house. When Shayna is busy or doesn't have any more to give, the girls help prepare meals for the family and work to carry on traditions from their childhood. The older boys babysit the younger boys and have taken on the role of wrestling and teasing. This hidden blessing of close-knit relationships will continue throughout the Kellers' lives as they grow and move in their own directions. They will always remember the tight bonds created during their formative years.

The family has since been compelled to turn to God. Shayna and Sam particularly discuss how Sam's illness has increased their faith in God and dependence on Him. Although things like family scripture study and prayer have become more difficult in light of Sam's illness, the rituals continue because they have learned the importance of doing these acts for their family. They want their children to grow up with faith that all things, even the hardest, work together for their good. The family is also more service oriented than they used to be, often loving and serving those less fortunate than they are. They have come to know and understand how such service can bless a life.

Sam and Shayna have learned to simplify their lives and their traditions. They have become more understanding and compassionate and less judgmental of others. They focus more on the parts of life that truly matter and have learned that they genuinely meant their marriage vows. Such discoveries are often hidden blessings in the intense crucibles families face.

# The Zales

Lorena and Matthew have grown closer together through Lorena's illness. Lorena's relationship with her father has also been strengthened through her trials. The age difference between Lorena and Matthew is another hidden blessing. Matthew is twenty years older than Lorena and is content with sitting still and caring for her. He no longer has a need to go on grand adventures or travel the globe. Like the Kellers, Matthew and Lorena "meant [their] marriage vows." Their complete fidelity to one another is a great blessing and comfort for Lorena. Lorena is active in several online support groups for those dealing with chronic pain and fatigue. Her involvement with these groups has been a huge blessing as it offers a sense of community even though she is unable to leave her home.

# The Goodsons

Sarah Goodson is surrounded by extended family. She moved closer to them at a time when she greatly needed extra love and support because Richard served far from home in the military. Although extended family is often a source of stress and fatigue for Sarah, she acknowledges them as a blessing as well. Her connections with neighbors and members of her congregation also serve as an incredible blessing in her life. Though many are unaware of her situation, she is aware of a few who battle similar situations. She offers support to them and they offer support to her.

Richard and Sarah have grown closer together through her illness, and both have really learned how to listen to and care for each other. They have come to value community and family at a deeper level. They report countless blessings from their involvement in church and community activities.

# The Clowards

Although Justin misses Jessica, he is happy she has found a purpose that keeps her focused and a step ahead of the depression constantly threatening to consume her and her family. She hopes her proactive role in the support community will be a blessing to her family as her children watch and learn to become involved in their communities. This is a lesson they did not learn before Jessica's diagnosis, but the children are all fairly involved in their respective communities now. It is a blessing for the family to have a cause to rally around.

Jessica listens better than she used to and has become more compassionate and extroverted. She strives to remember birthdays and important life events, something she didn't bother doing before. Jessica expresses gratitude because her children were mostly grown up before her diagnosis, and she recognizes this as one of the greatest blessings in her journey.

# The Swintons

People outside of the Swinton family may easily look at Kari and Adam's situation and believe her multiple sclerosis destroyed everything. After all, her marriage ended in divorce, her children still harbor frustration and resentment toward Adam and toward the changes her illness has caused, and her illness will only get progressively worse. Where are the blessings? Kari will be the first to show you the blessings. She has learned a great deal from her marriage with Adam and knows she will continue to learn from her illness.

Her unique attitude of looking for blessings in difficult situations helps her to find them quickly. Her diagnosis and divorce have taught her the importance of spending time together as a family. She plans to invest more energy in doing just that so her children will remain close to her. A family grows as they work through hard times together, and Kari is optimistic as she looks to the future and sees her family's potential for growth.

# The Franklins

Jennifer states, "I am very . . . blessed." She will tell you all about her blessings before she details the difficulties in her situation. She wants everyone to know there are blessings in trials and has made it her life quest to open her mouth and lift others. It's a guarantee: after visiting her, you will leave her home feeling optimistic about your future and better about yourself. She wasn't like that before her divorce and diagnosis of fibromyalgia. She is now active in the support community and reaches out in whatever ways she can. She was thrilled to be able to participate in Taralyn's thesis research and hopes it will help to lift and bless the lives of others.

Perhaps Jennifer's determination to remain close as a family in spite of life's curveballs is where her positivity stems from. She has done her job well; her family is closer to one another than many others. They are constantly together, and they are each other's greatest source of love and support. Jennifer would tell you her divorce and illness has made her a faithful, family-focused, forgiving, and strong person.

# Other "Families"

Taralyn heard the same request from her students nearly every night, "Sing sunshine." As Taralyn sang bedtime lullabies to her students at the boarding school, she knew she was giving them something special. They didn't have a mom around to tuck them in at night and tell them they were loved. She did those things. There were too many babies in the orphanage for the nuns to hold them while they drank their bottles. Taralyn did those things. There was too much work to be done for those kids to be played with or teased by their caretakers. Volunteers did those things. Taralyn and other volunteers came and went, but those children were blessed with loving, personalized attention. They knew, if only for a few moments, that somebody thought they were pretty special. They knew they were loved. As they grow into adulthood, they will remember the volunteers who helped to love and care for them in some of their darkest moments. They may not remember names, but they will remember how it felt to be so loved. Such love endures for a lifetime.

Amanda was known as "the terror." She had been in wilderness therapy for over one hundred days, a full month or two longer than most students. Every staff member dreaded being assigned to her group. Taralyn gulped when she saw that her name was written next to Amanda's group name on the assignment board. This particular group of students consisted of all girls, many who were tired of Amanda. Taralyn's anxiety over working with this group was only worsened as she visited with therapists and learned about some of the group dynamics. It was going to be a hard week. Something changed as Taralyn and her staff drove out to the group, though. Taralyn reread her notes from the therapist and began to see individual people instead of a terrifying group of catty girls. She determined she would treat them like people, not knowing what a difference that would make.

Amanda's therapist approached Taralyn at the end of the week, "What did you do differently than other staff? How did you reach her?" Taralyn responded, "I spent six hours brushing her hair." Amanda only brushed the ends of her hair, leaving the roots untouched. Imagine what one hundred days living in the wilderness without a proper washing or brushing can do to a head of hair! Administrators were threatening to cut off her hair to prevent disease and infection, and Amanda was mortified by the prospect. She begged Taralyn to help her, and Taralyn, seeing an individual needing help, agreed to help. They sat and brushed during breaks on hikes, while meals cooked, and while waiting for others to break camp. It took an entire week of incremental brushing, but by the end of the week, Taralyn had spent six hours brushing, twenty minutes washing, and twenty more minutes braiding Amanda's long blonde hair. Amanda had not received that much personalized attention for as long as she could remember, and she blossomed under Taralyn's care. As Taralyn brushed, they talked about Amanda's life and addictions, her relationships with others, and what was important to her. Her therapist called that week Amanda's turning point.

Similar scenarios played out every week in wilderness therapy. No teen would tell you living in the wilderness was a blessing initially, but by the end they all had a hard time saying goodbye. Sure they were excited to return home, see loved ones, and eat real food, but those situations were also scary. They had a new family in the wilderness, a family that loved them and knew them for who they really were without the drugs, alcohol, and other addictions. Unlike their own families, ghosts of addictive behaviors didn't haunt the people they left behind in the wilderness. They were so different now than the people they used to be. Would their families believe the changes were real? The blessings of wilderness therapy were often hidden, but endless. Those at-risk teens that thought there was no turning back had turned. Families reported having their child back again, free from drugs, alcohol, and other addictions. Staff became more loving and compassionate while working wilderness therapy.

There is always a silver lining. You just have to open your eyes to it. No matter your battle, gratitude for light in the midst of darkness heals wounds and erases scars. Darkness always loses to light. It was not always easy to see the good in trials we faced as a family. Ironically, Stuart is often the best at this, patiently waging his personal battles while constantly joking and helping the rest of us to count our blessings. As his light illuminated the darkness, our blessings became overwhelming. These trials have become our greatest asset as we have learned who the Clark family really is, what we stand for, and where our strength lies.

# CHAPTER 7

# It's Still Us

## "We're going to Disneyland."

The firmness in Stuart's declaration was a little unexpected. Sure, it sounds great . . . until you consider the long distance to drive and the resulting long stretches of sitting in a car. We knew what that would look like: the longer we drove, the more miserable Stuart would become. Muscle cramps, breathing issues, and pains were sure to follow. Not to mention Stuart could never endure all the walking that two theme parks required.

"That's what wheelchair rentals are for," Stuart countered.

"Sure, but what about [insert hardship here]?" we asked.

"We're going," he declared.

End of debate.

It's still us. Stuart is still the vision behind the adventures. They just look a little different now. We take more time to get started and we move a little more slowly, but Stuart still enjoys getting out to see the world. We have come to realize shutting down his desires simply because it all sounds too exhausting is never a good plan. If we shut the dream down, we shut him down. Pain and exhaustion still follow him everywhere, but he tries harder when he has chosen the adventure. We all know there will be a week or two of recovery after such epic journeys, but we have adapted to this cycle because it brings us all joy.

We still love movie nights and visiting Yellowstone. Movie marathons are too hard on Stuart, so now we just watch one. We drive through Yellowstone more than we walk the trails, but we are still there. Being sedentary has led to some interesting moments for Stuart. During a recent visit to Yellowstone, he was leaning against a fence while quietly observing a buffalo herd. He was motionless long enough that they no longer considered him a threat. In no time at all Stuart was surrounded. They were close enough for him to touch. A little disconcerting perhaps, but it was a thrill nonetheless. "Segway Man" had become the "Buffalo Whisperer." Adventure-filled memories still surround us.

Stuart's time spent in Thailand made Thai food part of our identity. Before his chronic issues, Stuart would create wonderful meals and invite the rest of us to partake of them. He still blends the magical flavors together, but now we all help slice, dice, and prepare the ingredients for his magic touch. People who come to visit our family are still gifted with this wonderful food, but now shared preparation is just as big a part of the experience.

As a family, we all work harder at creating memories and recording and sharing those memories time and again. If we are all together, there will be numerous cameras clicking away. When we are preparing to separate, there will be mandatory image file sharing before we say goodbye. As our family has evolved over the past decade, we have identified the traditions worth fighting for, the traditions that are worth extra required effort and sacrifice. They are still tied to who we were before, but they are adapted to who we are now. They exist because we have purposefully chosen to make them exist. Looking back is no longer about the way things were; it's about celebrating the journey we have traveled and all we have gained along the way. We are still the Clarks: an outdoorsy, God-fearing, fun-and-food-loving, tradition-keeping, loud, crazy, and active family.

# The Tidlunds

The Tidlund family continues to carry on the same traditions they always have, but those traditions have become more important to them. They know how quickly situations can change and do their best to provide memories and meaningful relationships for their children and extended family. They feel a sense of increased family strength after spending time together doing family scripture study, eating a meal together, or going on a family vacation.

Hadley's first trip back to the hospital to get an MRI became a family vacation. After her doctor visit, the family went to the zoo, ate out at restaurants, stayed in a hotel together, and visited sites important to their religious practice. Turning that first checkup into a fun memory has made further checkups less scary for the entire family. The Tidlunds have been through hard times. They may still battle fear occasionally, but they are still the Tidlunds: a family-focused, outdoorsy, faithful, trusting, spontaneous, and silly family.

# The Crandalls

Marcus and Julie's marriage ultimately did not survive. As such, Julie and Kassie are no longer a part of Marcus's daily life. The reasons for the collapse of their family unit are varied and go well beyond the season of trial brought on by Kassie's childhood leukemia, though key miscommunications can certainly be traced back to that time. Naturally, since the family lives in separate homes and states, much of their original family dynamic has changed. It would also be easy to assume they don't resemble at all who they were prior to Kassie's trial; it would be wrong to make such an assumption. In spite of Julie's emotional distance, she still holds a soft spot in her heart for her extended family because of the sacrifice and love that they showered on her struggling family during Kassie's illness. It's not unusual for her to commemorate the anniversary of such a visit with a heartfelt note.

Kassie still loves fantasy play. Her creative nature leads her to read and draw fantasy creatures and play elaborate fantasy video games. In spite of her geographic distance, Kassie consistently reaches out to her extended family through social media. Marcus and Kassie play hard when they are together. They especially enjoy being outdoors together. Marcus now knows he can turn to extended family when trials rear their heads once again, and he frequently does.

# The Kellers

The Kellers are still somewhat blinded by the newness of Sam's illness. When you ask them about their family pre- and post-illness, they will provide a list of changes and differences. From an outsider's perspective, however, the family looks largely the same. They continue to make family a top priority. Yes, traditions and celebrations are smaller than they once were, but they still happen. Yes, Sam often misses out on evening activities or morning scripture study, but those rituals still happen.

The kids have learned new ways to spend time with their dad. Rather than expecting him to take them on adventures, they spend more time with him at work. Rather than tackling him when he walks in the door, they cuddle up to him as he reads them a book. Yes, they now camp in cabins rather than tents, but they still go camping. They are slowly but surely learning ways to adapt and modify what matters most, so it still fits. Because we have been there, we know it will not be long before they can also declare, "It's still us!" For now, they focus on scaling back and accepting the chronic nature of Sam's condition. As they continue to adapt to each new situation Sam's illness creates, their family will grow stronger and become more solidified in who they are.

# The Zales

Lorena would tell you her family is fairly typical and just going through hard things—nothing special. There have been changes, of course. Matthew does all of the childcare, cooking, cleaning, and home repairs now. He supports the family financially and attends family events without Lorena. Family time is typically spent in pairs, but time is still intentionally spent together. Lorena Jand Matthew no longer play ice hockey, but they do spend time together watching television or reading books. The family no longer goes to the local park to play games, but they enjoy playing the Wii together in the comfort of their own home. Matthew wonders if the family wouldn't have been paired off even if Lorena were well. She doesn't do as well with teenage boys, and their son is a teenager now. They have certainly adapted, but they are essentially the same. In fact, they don't feel all that different anymore.

# The Goodsons

The Goodson family also does things in pairs rather than as an entire family, depending on how Sarah is feeling on any given day. When she is feeling well, the family continues to go on camping trips and do fun things together. Even if she's not feeling well, she can sit and watch a movie with the family or maybe even play a board game. She and Richard continue to go on dates frequently. Yes, Richard and their son have to step up and help more with house cleaning and cooking responsibilities, but their family is the same as it has always been.

# The Clowards

Jessica isn't able to spend as much time with her family in the evenings because there are too many stimuli for her to be comfortable, but she continues to spend time with her family in other ways. She often plays board games with Justin and their daughter who still lives at home. The family is mostly grown with families of their own now. As such, many of the changes have minimally impacted the kids. They all know their mom is an advocate for others battling illness, though, and rally with her in that cause. The family gathers together for weddings, and Jessica always remembers birthdays. If anything, Jessica's appreciation for her family has increased as she has waded through her journey with chronic illness.

# The Swintons

Kari fights tenaciously to maintain and strengthen her relationships with her children. Now more than ever, she understands how important those relationships can be. After her first divorce, the kids bounced between her home and her first husband's, which has created some distance in her relationships with them. She doesn't feel this has changed drastically since her diagnosis, though her children report some changes in the ways their mother responds to their needs and concerns. Her son maintains that his mom is incredibly kind and generous and states, "all my friends love her." Kari is determined to intentionally spend more time with her children and is hopeful that by doing so her family will grow closer together. Kari also continues to spend time with extended family and remains close to them.

# The Franklins

Jennifer doesn't want pity. Yes, things have changed, but her family is stronger because of the trials they have faced together. Although Jennifer is unable to get down on the floor and really play with her grandchildren as she did with her own children, she continues to play with them. She now sits in a chair and asks them to come to her, and they happily do just that. Her grandchildren love her, and they are her light. She is determined to provide a life of service and giving to others and starts with her own family. She takes joy in controlling what she can control; her home is immaculate and inviting. She is as active as she can be in her local support community for others struggling with chronic illness and hopes to help them as others have helped her. If you asked her friends about the Franklins, Jennifer believes you would hear something like, "She held it together. Wow." Jennifer just sees her family as normal.

# Other "Families"

Orphans become accustomed to constant transitions. They are moved from place to place, volunteers come and go, and rules change with each new caregiver. Yet the kids remain the same. A child with a sweet disposition maintains that disposition, while the child who likes to cause trouble with newcomers continues to cause trouble with newcomers. In adapting to the constant change in their lives, orphans develop a family identity in many ways. One thing is more constant than anything else: the other orphans. They become each other's siblings and cousins. When houses are moved around and they no longer live with the same children, they greet each other with joy upon meeting on the playground. When kids are adopted, they are greatly missed and constantly asked about by the other children. Even in the midst of constantly swirling change, these children find family and by doing so find a way to remain the same in spite of it all.

Graduation from wilderness therapy was a production. Parents hadn't seen their children for months. Those kids felt like they had lived in the wilderness for a lifetime; they claimed they learned more in two or three months than they had in most of their lives combined. They were strong and ready to face the future, addiction free. Strong but scared. Parents had heard positive things from their child's therapist, but how could such things be true? How could their child be completely reformed in just a few months? The problems had gone on for years. This change couldn't possibly stick; it was too good to be true. As these thoughts swirled through parents' heads, they looked up to see their child running full speed toward them. They hadn't seen that smile in years. Now their child was embracing them—he or she hadn't done that in years. Maybe this was real.

Parents would seek Taralyn and other staff out to say "Thank you. We feel like we have our son back." Those parents did have their child back. The change was real, but the challenges were just beginning. That child would go back home where he or she would face the same trials all over again. That child had doubts too. Will I be strong enough to maintain these changes? Do I want to maintain them? Will I be able to keep my cool when my parents aren't listening to me? Will I relapse? Some did relapse, but most didn't. The teens that were able to maintain changes made were the teens that had strong support from their families: families who were willing to adapt and change with their teenagers rather than expecting their teenagers to make all of the sacrifices. In that environment, yes, those changes were real. Those teenagers were the same as they had been in wilderness therapy.

Chemical reactions requiring intense heat are conducted in a crucible and result in a completely new product as the original materials are refined and transformed. Intense trials become such a crucible for families, resulting in refined and transformed family identities, though the result of any set of circumstances depends entirely on the choices of the family in the crucible. In spite of our stubborn tenacity, over time we truly became refined and transformed as a family. Our identity was simmered down to the bare essentials. We are the Clarks and we are a faithful, God-fearing family. We are strong and rely on each other. We know we can face and overcome anything because we have already done it. We love and serve the people around us because we know the power of angels. We spend time in work, play, and prayer together because those things help us to remember who we are and stay strong. Many families describe a similar refining transformation through crucible experiences. The addictions, illnesses, deaths, divorces, and other hard things families face help them to know and understand who they really are as a family. Identities are transformed and simplified. They are the same family, just a little clearer and more beautiful than they were before.

# CHAPTER 8

# Moving Forward

For a long time we looked for a return to normalcy. We would lay all our hopes on the next surgery, medication, or treatment as the magical missing piece that would make everything better. Good times would return when things were ordinary again. The danger of such a mindset is that you are going to be disappointed. We would hold our breath and wait for the return of normal routines, only to discover true normalcy is constant change.

Jennifer Franklin understood this: "Life is tough, but it's the life I have and I'm going to live it to the fullest." Likewise, Matthew Zale told Taralyn, "I guess what I've learned from it is . . . you don't go running off just because things don't turn out how you expect. It is what it is." Both Jennifer and Matthew know what we now know: there is no return to what once was. Yesterday is gone, but tomorrow is a new day. The trick to moving forward is to stand firmly in today and move toward tomorrow.

Sure, keep moving forward. We have all heard that one before. Add it to the list of cute phrases people tell you when they are just trying to make you feel better. They don't really understand what our family is facing. There is no moving forward from this! Wrong. As veterans of such reasoning, we stand ready to tell you those veins of reasoning are wrong.

We have already explained Taralyn's thesis research was conducted with families dealing with extraordinary challenges, but we haven't told you what Taralyn was hoping to find. Research shows one of two things happens when a parent is diagnosed with chronic illness or disability: family relationships either strengthen or weaken. Families either pull together while moving forward or they fall to pieces. There is no in-between. The purpose of her research was to discover why this dichotomy exists. Why are some families able to stick together and make it through while others simply cannot do so? There had to be a reason. Taralyn knew her family was closer than they were before the onset of Stuart's chronic illness. What had made her family strong?

While seeking out families to participate in her study, Taralyn met dozens of individuals and families battling illness and disability. She doesn't remember all of them, but she will never forget Christina. It was arguably the most difficult stage of Christina's illness: she had received her diagnosis of fibromyalgia but was still learning how to control her symptoms and face each new day. Her diagnosis was the last straw for her husband. He left. Chronic illness was not what he signed up for, and he was gone. It wasn't long before her teenage daughter followed in his footsteps. She was young, and it was just too hard to care for her mother, who was constantly depressed and in pain. Christina was left alone. What had made Christina's family fall to pieces so rapidly?

The more people Taralyn talked to, the more she realized the research was correct. Families were in various stages of pulling together or falling to pieces, but they were all facing one of those two scenarios. There was no in-between. Which direction is your family headed?

Taralyn's question took her all over the country in her quest to find answers. Her question led to some predictable answers and one that surprised her. Predictably, she learned all about family strength and what families do to intentionally or unintentionally build that strength in the midst of their crucibles. She also learned about family unity and what helped to maintain that unity. Unexpectedly, and perhaps most importantly, she also learned about the power of family story.

Research supports six characteristics of strong families. These six characteristics work together to create a web of family strength. As families work to strengthen one strand of that web, other strands are also affected. When one strand is weak or breaks, it doesn't take long for other strands to weaken and snap.

Appreciation for each other is the first of these characteristics. A day doesn't pass in our home without Stuart and Teresa expressing love for each other. "I love you" is said as people come and go, at the end of telephone calls, and before going to bed at night. There is no doubt our family loves each other.

"Thank you" is another phrase you are almost certain to hear while visiting our home. Thank you for the meal, the hug, the note. Thank you for helping me to figure out this difficult situation. Thank you for being you.

The strongest families in Taralyn's study also expressed appreciation for each other on a regular basis. Sam, Lorena, Jessica, Kari, Sarah, and Jennifer all expressed an immense amount of gratitude for those who cared for them on a daily basis. Other families also expressed appreciation for each other. Jennifer's daughter is "more grateful for the time [she has] left with [her] mom." Their family has become stronger because they are all grateful for this time. Sam's daughter is grateful for her family because they double as her "own fan section" at sporting events. Kari's "biggest joy of life is being a mom," and Jessica's children always acknowledge each other's increased talents and abilities. As families express appreciation for each other, they increase in commitment. Conversely, when families fail to express appreciation for each other, their web of strength begins to unravel. Perhaps this is where Marcus and Julie's unraveling began.

The second characteristic of strong families is commitment. The Kellers' and Zales' expressions of meaning their marriage vows are examples of strong commitment. In sickness or health, they promised to stand by each other and have done exactly that. Sarah Goodson will tell you they have stuck together as a family because "we're just so dedicated. Richard and I are dedicated to the family—to the marriage." Taralyn never remembers hearing her parents talk about divorce. When she was young, Teresa told her that she and Stuart had decided before they were ever married that they wouldn't even bring up the word. Divorce was not an option. Not all families in Taralyn's study expressed such strong commitment to each other.

The Swintons were not able to remain committed to each other in the end, resulting in divorce and separation. When Taralyn interviewed the family, Kari and Adam were balancing on the brink of divorce, and Kari's mother explained "I'm frustrated with the whole family because they don't help out like they should." Personal interests took root and their web began to unravel.

Spiritual wellness is the third characteristic that works to strengthen families. We are blessed with a family that is strong and active in our shared religion. We live our lives in accordance with the doctrines and principles taught therein. This choice makes us strong, provides hope in desperate times, and unifies our family. Half of the families in Taralyn's study shared their faith, while the other half varied by individual. Still, several of those families shared a common belief system such as the importance of serving others or the need for hope in the future.

Sam's thirteen-year-old son told Taralyn that "the gospel is the main thing that holds our family together. Without the gospel my mom might not even be married to my dad because it's so hard living with someone who's sick all the time and can't help out." Both Jessica and Jennifer attributed their emotional healing to the Lord, and Kari confesses the power of thought is amazing. Sharing in spiritual wellness helps families to cope, find meaning in crucibles such as illness, and stay strong in the face of future trials. Rifts in familial spiritual wellness begin weakening families as their interconnected webs start unraveling.

The fourth characteristic of family strength is spending time together as a family. Although chronic illness and other trials often drastically alter how families are able to spend time together, it is vitally important for them to continue to work and play with each other. Teresa feels the most supported by her children when they offer to paint a room, help out with some other home project, or help her take Stuart on adventures. Our family is consistently blessed as we spend time working, playing, and serving together. Hadley's tumor and Kassie's leukemia enabled both of their parents to come to understand the value of spending time together.

Though it is a challenge to find ways to spend time together when illness threatens to consume every moment, the effort is well worth it. Most of the families Taralyn worked with were more active prior to the diagnosis of chronic illness. Yet, they continued to spend time together. Sam said, "Even with the sickness we still have fun times," and Jessica stated, "Spending time together is very valuable. It gave my family opportunities to find our new normal." Families become stronger as they adapt to changes in their situation and still find ways to spend time with each other.

The fifth characteristic of family strength is developing ways to cope well with crises, such as the onset of chronic illness. Coping with the ever-changing variables in Stuart's health requires our family to constantly practice the coping skills we have developed over the years. As we are open and honest with each other about what we are feeling and experiencing, our family is able to cope with whatever life throws our way. All of the ill individuals Taralyn worked with learned to listen to their bodies and communicate their needs to family members. Jessica now feels joy when she feels tension or pain in her body because she knows what she needs to do to take care of herself. As families learn to cope well with illness, they begin to feel normal again. Jessica says, "My life feels so normal to me now, and I forget it's not." Maintaining flexibility in new situations and expressing hope in the future helps families to be strong. Each family finds different ways to cope with trying situations; the point is that finding what works for your family is essential if you hope to grow closer as a family through the vicissitudes of life.

The sixth and final characteristic of strong families is communicating effectively. Richard reports what keeps his family strong: "Probably communication more than anything . . . you can survive just about anything if you're talking to each other." Sam also states, "Communication does seem to be a strong glue binding our family together." Life's sucker punches often revolutionize the way families communicate with each other. We felt as if we had to learn a whole new language to be able to talk about what was happening with Stuart. As families work through the communication barriers created by trying situations, familial strength increases. And if they are unable to work through those barriers, that strength begins to unravel. The inability to communicate wants and needs effectively was a key contributor to the unraveling of Kari's marriage with Adam.

The families Taralyn visited certainly substantiated the six characteristics of strong families discussed in other research studies, but something was missing. There was a characteristic her families were talking about that didn't appear in the research: family unity. Although it was important for families to express appreciation for each other, be committed, be spiritually well, spend time together, cope well with crises, and communicate effectively, their webs of strength continued to unravel. Only when families were able to establish family unity did their strength solidify. In Taralyn's study, family unity was defined as a family acting as one, harmoniously working toward some goal or objective. Though Taralyn's research certainly justified a relationship between family unity and family strength, it is important to note no causal relationship can be determined without further research on the topic.

The six families in Taralyn's study talked about four key components of family unity. First, it was important for families to maintain a unified perspective. Although Taralyn and Taunalee were living at home during most of Stuart's worst years, it was challenging to get Tiffany and Steven on the same page. There is, after all, a big difference between living something and hearing about it through emails and telephone calls. Only after our first camping trip did the situation start sinking in for Tiffany and Steven. And only once our family saw Stuart's situation through the same eyes were we able to remain unified and strong in our battle. Jessica's family "knows the terrors of [her] illness." Likewise, each member of the Keller family could tell Taralyn exactly what Sam's illness was and how it was affecting their family. Marcus and Julie were unable to get on the same page in the way they viewed Kassie's situation, and Kari's daughter explained, "We all do different things, and we're all individual people in this family." Their inability to see through the same eyes diminished their unity and eventually their family strength.

Secondly, unified families shared common goals. Our family was determined to maintain our tradition of camping together. In many ways, this single-minded goal served to carry us through Stuart's most challenging years as we tenaciously fought to maintain our favored pastime. Common goals continue to unify our family and direct our paths. Jessica's illness itself served as a unifying factor as her family established common goals to strengthen others in similar situations. The Kellers' common goals before Sam's diagnosis carried on in spite of changes to family life. "Whatever my family does, we're good at it . . . my family doesn't accept average," Sam's sixteen-year-old daughter said. Other family members also refer to this shared goal of succeeding individually and as a family.

Common goals often center on family rituals and traditions. Shayna told Taralyn, "If you do it once, [the kids] think it's a tradition." The power of those traditions serves to unify families in meaningful ways. The lack of such goals and traditions serves to unravel families. Kari told Taralyn the Swintons "don't really have family traditions" or spend much time together. This lack of unity eventually tore their family to pieces.

Families are unified as they look beyond themselves and serve others. In many ways, the cancers and resulting deaths of Stuart's parents were a blessing for our family. Hadley's tumor was also a blessing in many ways. As these trials forced us to look beyond Stuart's illness, we became unified in loving and serving them, thereby strengthening our family. Taralyn's thesis research provided an opportunity for the families she worked with to serve others. Matthew told her, "I hope that we can be of help to you and eventually other families like us." Likewise, Jennifer was "glad [she had] a chance to help."

The Franklins and Clowards were both the most unified and altruistic in Taralyn's study. Jessica and Jennifer not only encouraged their families to be involved in serving others dealing with similar situations but also encouraged service in their religious communities. Families like Marcus and Julie's that became so absorbed by their own troubles were not unified or strong enough to withstand the pressures working to destroy them.

Finally, and most importantly for those in Taralyn's study, family story served as a unifying factor in their shared lives. All but one of the families in her thesis research were able to answer the question, "What is a story your family commonly tells?" All but one of the families in her research remained strong and unified through the chronic illness of a parent. When asked this question, Kari's daughter responded, "We don't usually have one story that we tell." Taralyn conducted interviews with five members of this family, and none of them were able to tell her a story. Kari seemed to recognize the importance of what she was saying as she fought back her emotions and told Taralyn she just couldn't think of a story right then. The inability to tell family stories set them apart from other families in Taralyn's study. Knowing the key stories of your family is incredibly powerful. They enable you to understand your family identity: learning from the past, living in the present, and looking hopefully toward the future no matter what life throws your way. Knowing who you are, where you came from, what matters, and where you're going is essential in moving forward while consistently abiding by established family standards. As new members join our family, the stories they hear help them understand our present as well as appreciate our past. Family story surrounds us. More and more the world is recognizing that the best way to share information is through a story.

While discussing the 2012 presidential election, a *National Review* magazine editorial stated, "Stories, not facts, are the way people process information. Screenplays, plays, scripts, and stories are packed not with hard data but with something more powerful and human: emotional data. That's why we remember stories long after we've forgotten facts. Stories stir our souls." The article goes on: "We're talking about the narrative of our nation. The story of America. The story of who we are, how we got here, and what we're to become." Telling those stories, they suggest, is key to helping others know who we are and where our passions lay.

We couldn't agree more. For families to be unified and have a truly rich identity, there are key stories they must know and tell themselves often. As families internalize their key identity stories, those around them will also gain a deeper understanding of who they are. Teresa recently reconnected with some long lost friends she hadn't seen in years. It was a delight to see them and reconnect. Having never experienced a high school reunion, she couldn't help but wonder if this joy was part of what she was missing. Of course, it should be noted that these reunions took place in a location where specific criteria determined who could enter. Because of those requirements, their unified presence meant they had all independently made similar lifestyle choices.

This did not mean Teresa knew what each of them had been through over the past several decades; it just informed her where they were in that moment. As Teresa shared experiences with these long-lost friends, she noticed an interesting phenomenon.

The first friend focused purely on the moment and joy of the reunion. The discussion was about personal light and appearance, and it was grounded solidly in the present. She and Teresa planned to meet again at a time and in a place where they could visit in depth for a longer period of time. They shared mutual enthusiasm for creating a new friendship in the present. On the other hand, the second friend downloaded a lifetime of trial in a matter of minutes. Every bit of information shared was tied to heartache of some kind. As other mutual friends from long ago were discussed, their tragedies were also shared. The discussion was heartfelt and joyful, yet the information weighed heavily on Teresa's heart. Uncharacteristically, she even found herself drawn into sharing some trials of her own.

The saying "You reap what you sow" comes to mind. These two experiences stand in stark contrast to one another. Both involved a joyful reunion and an obvious understanding of renewed trust. Yet Teresa's perceptions of these beloved friends were greatly influenced by what they chose to share. Their perceptions of her were greatly influenced by what she chose to share in response to them. We have experienced within our own lives the power of telling a positive story. The way we view our situation and share it with the world informs our psyches on a cellular level. Are we victims? Are we heroes? Are we triumphant? Are we overburdened? We physically respond to the stories we tell ourselves in very powerful ways. Pain and trials are real, but how we deal with them in our own heads has a powerful influence on how our bodies react. So it is with friendships.

This experience reinforces our desire to tell the stories of our success. We want our hearts to believe our words. We want other people to believe our hearts. What story do your words tell about you? Through Teresa's work as a professional storyteller, she has identified seven key identity story themes every family should know and share: sacred stories, creation stories, origin stories, gratitude stories, success stories, family shorthand, and divinely directed diversions. These stories illustrate just who a family is, how they got to where they are, and what they want to become.

A creation story is the story of how your family came to be as it is today. Usually epics, these stories may not be simple, but they are key to who you are. They define how you see yourself in addition to how the world sees you. In a very real way, this book is our creation story. Other creation stories for our family would include events such as how Teresa and Stuart fell in love, the birth of every child, the courtship of each married child, or the birth of every grandchild. A family creation story is born every time there is a new beginning. A unified foundation for family identity is created as families grow and purposefully remember and share these stories.

Matthew and Lorena Zale love telling the story of how they met and married. They were both physically active and ended up on the same ice hockey team. As such, they thought a wedding on ice was in order. Lorena wore a purple Victorian style dress and her ice skates, and Matthew was dressed to match. Their ceremony was the first for the newly inaugurated mayor of their city, a fact the Zales proudly announce. Lorena always wanted to have children but was unable to do so. The story of how they adopted their son is another piece of their creation story.

Most couples love telling the stories of how they met, married, and created their families. In fact, Taralyn heard the creation stories of every family she met while conducting her thesis research, and our family can tell you creation stories for several generations back. Creation stories help us to remember who we are and how we started. They keep us grounded when everything else seems to be swirling around us.

So how was your family created? Has the story changed over time? Have you reinvented your family, or does the original creation story tell the full tale?

Your origin story is the story of who and where your family comes from. In other words, origin stories are the stories of your ancestors. The Zales and Franklins both told Taralyn origin stories as she visited with their families.

Matthew's Russian Jewish ancestors immigrated to America to find a better life, free from religious persecutions. Jennifer's father and uncle were both interested in dating the same girl. So, her father locked his brother up in a closet while he took this beautiful girl on their first date. The girl later became his wife and Jennifer's mother. These stories help children and grandchildren know who they are and what they have inside of them. Knowing the cultures and traditions of the people you descend from opens up eyes of understanding to family traits, convictions, and interests. Core identity can be strengthened and enhanced by knowing the trials your ancestors have faced. In fact, studies show youth are less likely to act out or contemplate suicide when they know the stories of their families.

For example, we come from a long line of intrepid pioneers. We have identified numerous ancestors who left their homes of comfort in Europe and Eastern America to haul handcarts or join wagon trains coming to the West. Knowing these stories has helped us face challenges time and again.

Mary Branagan left Ireland at the age of eighteen to come to Utah. She pulled a handcart from Florence, Nebraska, all the way to Salt Lake City, Utah. Mary Branagan (known by her friends and family as Molly) was a well-bred Irish lass who had chosen to join a church against her parents' wishes. She had snuck off to be baptized without telling anyone and thought she'd gotten away with it until her sister confronted her. Molly swore her little sister into secrecy and testified to her that she believed she had found the gospel of Jesus Christ in its purest form on the earth. That's when Molly's sister begged her not to leave to join the Latter-day Saints at their Zion in Utah. What was Molly's response? "I'll do whatever the Lord asks of me."

Molly did travel across the sea and plains of America to Utah. But first she had to arrange for her travel. When her father discovered her plans, she was locked in her bedroom for three months. She eventually found ways to sneak out to smuggle her clothing and money to a safe house so she would be ready for the journey. The day the ship left Ireland, she hadn't realized it was her last day in her beloved homeland. She had slipped out of the house with more clothes, but when she arrived at the place she'd been storing supplies, they declared the ship was leaving that very hour. She rushed off, never saying goodbye to her family, never to see them again. When she arrived in Florence, Iowa, she discovered she would be pulling a handcart across the plains. She was limited to a mere seventeen pounds of personal possessions due to the limited space. She had to set aside much of the clothing she'd worked so hard to sneak out of the house to bring to America.

Molly was quite sure her pampered hands couldn't take such a journey, so she got her handcart and "hired a good strong man to pull it." The first day of their trek west, a windstorm blew dust in their faces all day long. It was a forbidding way to start such a journey. The "good strong man" she'd hired ditched out and took her handcart with him. Suddenly, Molly found herself alone on the plains of America, with nothing to her name but the clothes on her back.

What was she to do? That's exactly what her pioneer company captain asked her when he found her standing alone and sobbing her heart out in a grove of trees. Molly swallowed hard and declared, "Why, exactly what I set out do to. I'll get myself a handcart and God willing, I'll pull it right on to Zion."

"Why you plucky little thing," her captain responded, "You are the girl I thought you to be; I believe you will." Molly got her handcart and was loaned a blanket and some cooking supplies.

Molly's story became a lighthouse for Teresa to turn to again and again. A shattered ankle requires a lot of time to heal. Stuart spent the time helpless in a chair, like an overseer supervising the family. It wasn't his intent, but that's how it felt sometimes. We set him up in the living room so he could be in the throes of the comings and goings of our lives. For all intents and purposes, he looked fully engaged, but there were distinct differences. About two weeks after he got home from the hospital, Stuart and Teresa's oldest daughter failed to come home by curfew.

She didn't call home, and Teresa's concern mounted with each passing hour. She woke Stuart up, begging him to search with her for their daughter. He informed her that his pain was too great. He would be unable to help in any way. Getting into the car would be too difficult. Teresa left to search alone. She didn't find her daughter (though her daughter eventually made it home safely with an interesting tale of her own early the next morning). It seemed Teresa's predawn drive had very little to do with her and a great deal to do with the Lord getting her alone in a place where she would listen.

It was during that fear-filled, early-morning drive that she began to think of Molly and her handcart. It was during this drive God patiently let Teresa know she was loved, but she would be pulling the cart alone. There was no "good strong man" to help pull it. But it was during this drive in the darkest moment before the dawn when the Lord tenderly reminded her He had given her the courage she needed for her trek through the chronic illness that lay before her. She was armed with family story.

For the nineteenth-century handcart experiment to be successful, there had to be firm criteria in place, such as the make, model, and dimensions of the cart. Additionally, there was a seventeen-pound weight limit per person. That's how much each person could place in the cart: seventeen pounds of personal possessions. Try winnowing down your personal possessions for a three-month journey to seventeen pounds; it's pretty easy to hit that weight rather quickly! A change of clothes and a blanket almost reaches the maximum. Add a book or cherished trinket, maybe a sack of seeds, and you're there. Molly's personal possession weight had been decreased to nothing with the absconding of her handcart. However, before that fateful night, she had faced the difficult choice of limiting her selection of personal possessions to seventeen pounds. As a daughter of privilege, she had many fine items, much of which had been carefully set aside and left behind when her handcart company headed out. Her valued possessions had made the journey to America but would not make the journey to Utah. Seventeen pounds became Teresa's personal metaphor. If she was going to haul her husband in a handcart over a rolling, dusty trail stretching as far as the eye could see, she was going to have to weigh in every day. She recognized dealing with limitations due to the chronic illness would be the first step to survival.

Molly would declare her journey west was one of the grandest times of her life, except for some hunger. Two incidents from her story burned themselves into Teresa's soul. The first occurred late in August on the high plains of Wyoming. The company had been promised they would not have to cross any more streams or rivers that day. This was a great relief to Molly, as the wind was getting cold, and crossing meant getting her feet and petticoats wet. She would cross barefoot with her shoes and socks hung around her neck so they would remain dry, but waist down she was sure to be wet. With the chilling wind and lateness of the day, a river crossing was sure to make for a miserable and damp night. That's why Molly put her foot down when the call went out to cross the river.

She was not going to cross another river that late in the day. Her leaders must keep their word. To emphasize her determination, she stepped out of the traces of the cart and folded her arms defiantly. It was obvious there would be no reasoning with her, so her captain simply picked her up, tossed her into the handcart, and pulled her across the river himself. He then unceremoniously dumped her out on the other side and walked away. That night a blizzard blew into camp. They were camped in a grove of trees, so they were able to get enough wood to keep fires going and fend off the freezing clutches of death that night. On the side of the river Molly had refused to leave, there were no trees or deadfall of any kind. They would have had a completely different outcome had they stayed on the other side of the river.

Shortly after that bitterly cold night, they reached Fort Bridger, and her captain brought her a fine pair of moccasins. "Why, whatever will I do with these?" Molly questioned. "I have no money to pay for them, and I won't be entering the Valley of Salt Lake in debt!" Her captain was stunned by her response. Surely, he reasoned, her shoes had worn out like all the others, and she'd be grateful not to walk another day barefoot through the sage. A radiant smile spread across Molly's face as she lifted up her skirts and displayed her well-constructed and fully-soled shoes. "Perhaps, sir, [the others] haven't prayed over their shoes each night as I have?" Molly had a fear of going barefoot, so she had desperately prayed each night that her shoes would not wear out until she could afford new ones. Her shoes lasted all the way to the valley and through the first winter. Molly's stories lifted Teresa again and again. Plans change and storms come, but prayers extend capacity and are truly answered. Weigh in the handcart. Stick to the trail. Put one foot in front of the other and the joy will come.

For some inexplicable reason, as Stuart regained his mobility and returned to work, we decided it was a good time to redo the kitchen. Stuart needed a project. Losing a parent is beyond difficult. Stuart described it best: "It's a powerful shift in the force." Having plans to draw, cupboards to pull down, soffits and walls to destroy, and appliances to pull was exactly what he needed to work out his angst over the slow passing of his father. Stuart was absolutely helpless to do anything to stem the slow degradation to death. Having something to take apart kept his hands and mind busy. Of course, there were also some days that it was all too overwhelming.

Through breathtaking personal experience, we have experienced that anesthesia can have a depressive effect. Long after the surgery is over and you recover, you still feel slightly off. Joy is fuzzy. Emotions feel different. Short-term memory is shot. Now, overlay that with a dying parent. It really didn't surprise us that some days were just too hard to get through. Home improvement could wait.

Mankind is interesting. Humans seem to have an innate need to analyze and qualify one another. It's so easy to sit back and observe one another, deciding how we would handle each other's situations if we were in charge. It's quite another experience to live through those situations. We had lived in our home for thirteen years surrounded by good neighbors and friends. There had been plenty of times we had helped one another through trials. For some reason, this was different. Rumors started to float back to us. People were judging us. Stuart was taking too long to recover. We were spending too much time in Utah. Teresa should kick Stuart in the behind and make him finish the kitchen immediately. Months had passed. Summer wasn't going to last forever. What would we do when winter came, and we could no longer cook with the camp stove on the deck? How long were we going to allow dishes to be done in the bathtub?

Suddenly, Teresa began to understand how Molly felt the morning she woke up and discovered her handcart and all of her worldly possessions were gone. She had been asked to pull the handcart alone. Should Teresa really be surprised? Don't misunderstand. We had a few deeply trusted friends who helped us in spite of the naysayers. We were not left comfortless, but we were left to meander a little aimlessly while we looked for our trail. Yet Molly's story had prepared us for the darkness of this storm. Teresa knew she could find light in the midst of her desperate prayerful pleading.

When you stand on the open prairie of the high plains in Wyoming and look across the Mormon Trail from the side, you can't see it. The grasses and sage are high enough that you simply can't see the ruts of the trail until you are on them. But when you stand on the trail and look behind you, the trail can be seen for miles. It's the same if you look forward. The time had come for Teresa to stop looking at our situation from the side as if it would suddenly change and return to normal. Nothing would ever be the same again. Teresa needed to place herself fully on the trail so she could see where we were all heading. She needed to start pulling the cart rather than just stand by it. That's the power of knowing the origin stories in your family.

Think about your ancestors. Who are they? Where do they come from? What did they do that inspires you? How do you remember and honor the sacrifices found in your heritage?

Sacred stories are just that: stories that represent all your family holds sacred. They are the beliefs that stir your souls and encourage you to try harder. These are the stories you turn to when you need to be reminded that sacrifice is faith in process. These aren't necessarily the stories outsiders will hear because they are special and should be guarded. There is no need to expose the sacred to outside critique. However, that does not mean they shouldn't be identified and repeated often within the family. These are the stories that cause a feeling of reverence in your heart. It is important to share moments of tender mercy when help came in miraculous ways.

"I haven't felt like myself in years." Ever since Stuart had lived in Thailand he had told people that. Something was off and no one believed him. When the cascade of medical issues began, he would repeat that declaration. He began to collect quite the team of physicians; each was focused on a specific symptom, but none were looking at the whole. Teresa began to believe there was something being missed that was seriously wrong, but her concerns were dismissed. One weekend, Teresa, Stuart, and his mother, Carol, went for a visit to Arizona. The high altitude took a toll on both Stuart and Carol. Teresa woke up in the hotel one night, gasping for breath. Both Carol and Stuart had their oxygen concentrators on the highest settings. They may have been getting all the oxygen they needed, but Teresa's air was awfully thin. She stumbled to the window and opened it, taking in deep chilly breaths of mountain air as tears streamed down her cheeks.

"Help me God, please," she prayerfully gasped. "What are we missing? Stuart is getting worse." By the time they were driving home, Stuart was nearly incoherent. Later, in the emergency room, a mass was found in Stuart's lungs. There was talk of cracking open Stuart's chest for a biopsy, but there was concern he wouldn't survive the procedure. His medical team was consulted, and none knew clearly what step to take. That's when Teresa felt a rush of courage and a prompting within her heart to repeat what she had cried out to God a few nights before: "We're missing something."

The room grew silent as the doctor considered her statement. Then he declared, "Perhaps you're right. I'm stumped. I'm sending Stuart to the best infectious disease specialist I know." The new doctor was a miracle. She spent hours with Teresa and Stuart, collecting a full life history of every place they had ever visited and every illness Stuart had ever experienced. She listened intently as he shared his concerns about Thailand. Ultimately, she ordered a full spectrum of tests and uncovered the reality that Stuart had contracted an insidious disease (melioidosis) in Thailand thirty years previously. It had a 90 percent morbidity rate. It frequently lays dormant, waiting to strike decades later. Some Vietnam vets refer to it as "the sleeping dragon." On average, only five cases a year are diagnosed in the United States. Stuart was failing fast. Immediate, intensive, and successful treatment followed.

The miracle was that this new doctor listened. The right person at the right time had been placed in Stuart's path. He had seen infectious disease specialists before and none had ordered the proper tests. The sacredness of this tale is that Teresa was prompted to repeat herself. The tender mercy was that the doctor had listened and stepped out of the way. This sacred moment, shared often within our family, strengthens the courage and faith of us all.

What are your sacred moments? Can your family tell them to each other?

Family shorthand consists of the stories only your family will understand. Families speak in shorthand. Shayna Keller keeps a book dedicated to their family shorthand: funny quips that get the whole family laughing. Now they say things about the stories, keywords like "ham sandwich," that make the family laugh and bring them closer together. They like to tease each other. Shayna says, "writing them down makes them live." She told Taralyn some of their family shorthand. For example, a daughter went to a luau and was disgusted by the roasted pig; she vowed to never eat pork again. That night for dinner they were eating ribs and she asked, "Is this pig?!" When they told her it was, she replied, "I'm not eating this. I'm going to eat a ham sandwich!" Families have a special code. In less than ten words we can remind everyone present of an epic event from our past. Be it funny, sacred, or somewhere in between, we all do it. It can be tough to be an outsider dropped into a Clark family gathering because they are lost and shut out when the shorthand starts flying. It's rarely intentional, but since shorthand is a habit this situation can occur frequently. When we can recognize the tales that have collapsed into shorthand, our ability to welcome others into our family is improved. By sharing the back story behind the shorthand we ensure everyone in the room understands.

"There's my beast!"

"I looove Guacamole."

"Are there bears in Bear World?"

"Is that supposed to look like a wagon wheel?"

"I see the grand croutons!"

"Tell us a story, you toot little man."

These sentences mean nothing to the rest of the world, but they mean the entire world to us. Each one triggers a story from our family lexicon. Smiles cross our faces, knowing glances are exchanged.

Teresa saw the evidence of family shorthand firsthand in a workshop she presented to nine sisters. The youngest and oldest were twenty years apart. Though these women had grown up with the same parents and in the same home, their experiences had been vastly different. For years the older sisters had assumed the youngest understood the shorthand. Yet during all those years she had felt shut out, assuming the distance was because she was the youngest and they didn't care as much. As the workshop unfolded, the older sisters began to flesh out the stories behind the shorthand. Each time they did, newfound understanding flashed across the youngest sister's face. At the end of the workshop, all of the sisters confessed they had never spent time talking like that. They felt as if their relationships were freshened and renewed. They realized there was much they didn't know about each other, and they left vowing to create more opportunities to share in the future. The youngest sister declared, "This is great. I actually feel like I'm one of them now."

Essentially, we're telling you to be purposeful in the way you interact as a family. Knowing the shorthand and when it needs to be expounded is vital to welcoming others into the bosom of your family. We recently experienced this in our own family. Four generations of our family traveled hundreds of miles to gather in Tiffany's home; seventeen people were under the same roof with just one bathroom. (Now there's a story!) Taunalee brought along her new best friend and would be husband, Peter, and introduced him to the family en masse! It was a loud, crazy, and fun event filled with laughter, great food, and great stories. We loved every minute of it, but one of the things we cherish most was watching everyone share our family stories with Peter. It wasn't performance based at all, but rather a natural outpouring of explanation and joy. Each time the shorthand came out, someone would pause to share the back story. It was a tremendous way for Peter to hear classic family stories and a delightful way to embrace him as part of the fold. It is through the family stories we choose to share repeatedly amongst ourselves that our identity as a family is solidified. Listen for your family shorthand. Does everyone in your family know the back story?

Stories of gratitude may just bring a tear to the eye. Obviously, the list of what your family is most grateful for can change on any given day, but if you think about it long enough, you will identify key aspects that you are always thankful for. Not every moment of gratitude brings a tear to the eye or elicits an emotional response. Simple little moments can inspire feelings of gratitude.

Even trials can have this effect. No one determines what you are thankful for, but the story of why you are thankful may be exactly what your family needs. Stuart's insistence to work the swing shift is a gratitude story in our family.

An excellent example of the lasting impact gratitude stories can have on the generations of a family was played out recently in ours. Teresa has a great-great-grandma Tobitha, who was born in 1834. As a young girl in Illinois in the 1840s, she was orphaned and ultimately driven from her home due to religious persecution. As a result, she drove an oxcart across the plains at the age of twelve. As Teresa grew up, she was quite grateful for this example of strength in the midst of adversity. Later, as an adult, Teresa spent a year researching and developing a performance story about Tobitha's life. Consequently, her children grew up knowing even more about this grandma and had even more reason to be thankful for her tenacity and for the legacy she left behind for her family.

Part of that legacy can be found in the historical community of Nauvoo, Illinois. Taunalee chose to be married in Nauvoo because of this multigenerational gratitude for a young girl and other ancestors who stood up for what they believed. This letter, written the week of Taunalee's wedding, illustrates the impact of lasting gratitude.

> *Dear Grandma,*
> *Today, I will close the circle you began oh so long ago.*
> *Today, I will marry the man I love in the building you sacrificed to create.*
> *Today, I will celebrate in the village your young eyes saw destroyed.*
> *Today, I will walk where you walked, because your courage led the way.*
> *Today, I will feel you closer than ever before, because I know your story.*

Taunalee's story is a pretty remarkable illustration of the impact an oft-told story of gratitude can have on generations. Knowing and frequently reviewing family gratitude stories will strengthen not only your immediate family but generations to come. While four generations of our family were gathered at Tiffany's home for Thanksgiving, we took some time to discuss what we were most grateful for. None of us will forget the thoughts shared that day. And if we do, Tiffany has it on video!

What is your family most grateful for? What are you grateful for? Have you told your family lately?

Stories of divinely directed diversions require making plans but embracing realities. Just what is a divinely directed diversion? It is the concept that providence uses outside forces or moments of trial to direct us off our chosen path to acquire all we need in order to be prepared for what we will be required to do.

Taralyn was quite proud in announcing, "I received my bachelor's degree in three and a half years so I could start my graduate studies in a timely manner." With an associate's degree in international studies and a bachelor's degree in sociology with a minor in Chinese, Taralyn planned to get her master's degree in marriage and family therapy before entering the field of international adoption. She had already spent a semester teaching children abroad and had no doubts. Her plan was perfect, but life threw her a curveball. She should have known it was coming; this always seemed to happen when she made plans.

She wasn't accepted into the graduate school of her choice. In fact, she wasn't accepted anywhere. While her academic record was stellar, she was deemed too young and inexperienced. Sucker punched; Taralyn was lost. She only had one plan and now that path was blocked. Forced to look at other options, she found a want ad for staff at a wilderness rehabilitation program. Taralyn loved the outdoors, but backpacking, hiking for miles in the wilderness, and going a week between showers was not her idea of a dream job. Nevertheless, she felt compelled to apply. That choice dramatically altered everything.

Taralyn often refers to that job as her "wilderness makeover." The Taralyn who showed up for staff training was a completely different person than the Taralyn who returned home after two years on the job. Her work with fellow staff and at-risk teens threw everything she knew and believed into question. Pre-wilderness therapy, Taralyn thought she knew everything and could conquer anything life threw at her. Post-wilderness therapy, Taralyn knew she had much to learn and knew she could accomplish anything with help from the Lord. Teenagers in wilderness programs are not the only ones whose lives are changed by the venture. Taralyn wrote several poems during her wilderness therapy stint:

"I came here to help others, to see others change their lives. Me, I had no problems . . . I almost feel superior. Like a hero stepping in to find lost souls and save them from the pits they've fallen in . . . I get paid to witness miracles . . . My life has been transformed . . . I no longer feel superior. I realize now what I've always said: Everyone has room to grow, everyone has things to change, and everyone is beautiful . . . The wilderness has transformed me into something better, stronger, and deeper . . . There are no completed projects and I need a lot of work, but thank you to the wilderness, to the people and the places. For now my eyes are open wider than they've ever been."

Divinely directed diversion. Nobody could have told Taralyn where God would lead her when she graduated from college. She wouldn't have believed them anyway. She had her plan. God had His plan, too. He knew what it would take for her to learn to follow His plan for her. After a few years of working in wilderness therapy, Taralyn knew it was time to return home. She didn't know where she was going, but she knew it was time to go. As she sang to a group of at-risk teens one last time that night as they curled up in their sleeping bags in the middle of nowhere, she sang about what was coming next in her life: "Lead kindly light . . . Keep thou my feet, I do not ask to see the distant scene—one step enough for me. I was not ever thus, nor prayed that thou shouldst lead me on. I loved to choose and see my path; but now, lead thou me on!"

Taralyn returned home with no plan in place, a first for her. Her return was heaven-sent, albeit short-lived. She was able to help Teresa around the house and work as the assistant director of a local summer camp. It was almost as if now that she had received her formal education, God was giving her an education of His own. Step one: wilderness makeover. Step two: camp management experience. It was less than a year before Taralyn knew it was time to move on. She left the country for three months to volunteer in orphanages, where she would once again attempt to make plans. Step three: help Taralyn understand the importance of family.

She had a plan in place again. Not really because the plan felt right, mostly because she just wanted a plan. Well, it didn't feel wrong either. She was an adult and would not move home again. Nope, not happening. She would get her master's degree in social work and get on with her life. But first she went home for the holidays.

Taralyn didn't leave home after the holidays ended. Stuart's health had plummeted while Taralyn was abroad, and she knew without a shadow of a doubt she was needed at home. The next year and a half would rekindle her memories of the importance of family. It would deepen her ties to her parents and teach her what marriage was all about. Her concurrent administrative experience at a local residential drug and alcohol rehabilitation program for at-risk youth would remind her of buried frustrations from her work in wilderness therapy.

Teens in rehabilitative settings make incredible changes. Granted, they are not always genuine, but they are incredible nonetheless. Taralyn loved working with at-risk teens but always harbored frustration. After they finished the program, they would go back to parents and siblings who also needed to be rehabilitated. Families would fall into the same patterns of communication—the same follies—and their children would relapse. Taralyn came to believe something about treatment programs must be broken, since they didn't seem to work anyway. As a result, she felt called to a new quest.

Taralyn once again planned to continue her education, though this time she knew it was inspired. She could feel God directing her as she searched for a program that would enable her to take a family approach to treating addiction. When she found Brigham Young University's master's program in youth and family recreation, she knew it was right. Away she went with new plans. She would work to establish her own camp: a facility where families would come together to learn necessary skills and heal from hurts. She was getting closer, but God had more for her to learn.

Taralyn was blessed to live with Grandma Clark during the first year of her graduate studies and was profoundly influenced by the gift of being Grandma's caretaker. When she didn't have other matters to think about, her mind was constantly wandering to Grandma and Stuart. Perhaps that's why a particular article stuck out. As soon as she read it, she knew her path had changed again. The article detailed the ways the limitations of disabled children impacted family leisure pursuits.

Taralyn's thesis research was born. She learned more over the next three years than she ever thought possible and describes the experience as trying to drink from a firefighter's hose. Her thesis research and success in graduate school led to several universities recruiting her for doctoral research. Again, with Taralyn's plan in place and bags packed, God opened a different door. Taralyn had learned God's plan was better, so she dropped her bags and stepped through.

This series of divinely directed diversions led Taralyn to a career she had not anticipated but loves with all her heart. Such stories remind families that sometimes the curveballs and speed bumps along the way can have a greater meaning than we realize. They encourage us to keep our eyes wide open in the midst of the sucker punch because we never know when the impact will open a new and better path before us.

What divinely directed diversions are found in your family?

Finally, we must know and tell our stories of success. In an article published in *The Wall Street Journal* (reported in the midst of economic turmoil), teens actually yearned to hear the stories of their ancestor's depression-era families and how they overcame difficulty and survived. Knowing these stories of success empowered them when they were faced with their own trials. Success isn't only found in our ancestor's lives. It can be found at the big game when your brother shot the winning ball through the hoop just as the buzzer sounded. It can be remembering the rolls that turned out just right when you made them for your mother-in-law. And it can even be found in remembering how the family all laughed instead of cried the night one very sick and confused grandpa ate sour cream by the spoonful.

When we asked our extended family to share a success story, they all came up with something different: getting out of debt, my five-year-old talking in school, my daughter survived a brain tumor, I got the role I wanted in the school play, I soloed on the mountain for a week, I survived my ankle fusion, I graduated from college after thirty years and four different attempts, we sky dove on our honeymoon, our kids are well behaved in other's homes, we landscaped our yard, I flew to Florida by myself and didn't get lost, everyone attended our first reunion in spite of the short notice, I made her laugh every day. Of course, we recognize this list may not make much sense to you, but because we know the back stories, this list fills our hearts with pride and emotion. We commonly share stories of success in our family.

The list goes on and on. However, we often forget to create the list in the busy rush of our lives. Just as taking inventory in a retail store reminds a storekeeper of all they have in stock, knowing the success stories within your family reminds you of everything you've accomplished. You can do this because (insert name here) overcame that. Keeping track of triumphant moments creates a list of inspiring stories for the next time someone needs a lift.

What does success look like in your family? Does your family have a list?

Can you feel the power of our stories? Coauthoring this book has been a challenging venture. It is one thing to sit down and write a book; it is quite another to sit down and write a book with someone that lives in a different state. We were certain of one outcome when we started, though. This book would be written in story. Consequently, we never set out to provide you with a "to-do list" book designed to help you build your family strength and maintain a unified front. In truth, a lot of people don't like reading books full of to-do lists! Those kinds of lists work best when you write your own, anyway. So what will you do next?

# Appendix

"I remember that, really, I do!" Taunalee was eight years old in 1998. It would be easy to assume she never knew the father Tiffany, Taralyn, and Steven knew. Yet time and again she declares she has a memory of the events her siblings are talking about. She was so small during much of those early experiences, how could that be possible? When a story is told several things happen to the listener. Memories are triggered like a cascade of images marching through the listener's mind. These memories are joined with the images conjured through the words of the one telling the story. Everything becomes fresh and is stored within the listener's mind as if it is a recent memory. When multiple family members share their own versions of the tale and photographs are viewed, the memory magnifies and deepens for the listeners. Through intentional and frequent sharing, the listener assimilates memories and experiences in deeply powerful ways. In truth, they may have been too little to remember such events on their own, but growing up surrounded by such stories ingrains the memories in their minds and hearts as well.

Taralyn has experienced this firsthand in many of her places of employment. Aspen Grove Family Camp celebrated their fiftieth anniversary in 2013, and Taralyn swears she has fifty years of memories although she only began her work there in 2011. As she has looked at old photographs and listened to the stories of those who have served at Aspen Grove much longer than she has, fifty years worth of stories have become a part of her. Go visit Aspen Grove. She would be happy to give you a tour and share those stories and memories with you, and you would never guess which ones are not her own.

This is not a new idea, but it is one modern society has strayed from. Many ancient civilizations intentionally created a culture where the eldest members of the village cared for the youngest members of the village so the children would know the stories of their people. In this way the children grew up filled with the memories, stories, and culture of their people as if they had experienced it all themselves. When families are scattered over great distances, such a culture is hard to create. But it can be done, and it is important.

So how do you create such a story-rich family culture? A good place to start is to take some time looking at where you stand today. We created these questions to help you do just that.

- Can you describe your family identity in ten words or less? Write them down.
- How often does your family admit and discuss family struggles?
- Does your family honestly acknowledge expressing attitudes that exclude outsiders? (Exclusion meaning your tendency to keep trials to yourself. Or in other words, do you assume no one else will understand, so you just suffer in silence?)
- In what ways does your family express appreciation for helpers?
- How often does your family count its blessings?
- Does your family remain true to your core identity in spite of trials faced?
- What does success look like in your family?
- What family stories does your family commonly tell?

As you ponder these questions, you may be able to identify where your web of family strength and unity may be weak or fraying. Now you should know what core family-identity stories will help you in times of turmoil. The next step is to create opportunities to remember and share those core family-identity stories.

Creation :: Origin :: Sacred :: Shorthand :: Gratitude ::
Divinely Directed Diversions :: Success

By way of review, there are key stories families must know and tell themselves often in order to be unified and have a truly rich identity. Now that you know what stories you need your family to cherish, how do you intentionally remember, craft, and share them? It starts at home, of course. You need to get people talking. There are hidden benefits to the harvesting and sharing of family stories. Not only are relationships strengthened and identities enhanced, but reading, writing, and public speaking skills are also magnified. Before we outline some action steps for your family, we would like to quickly review what a story is.

Our story within this book follows the classic story arc. In the classic story arc, or hero's journey, someone receives an unexpected task he or she must accomplish. As said someone embarks on the journey, he or she meets helpers along the way, and together they accomplish the task. With the completion of the task, they either return to their normal activities with a deeper understanding or with an actual item reminding them of what they have accomplished. Classic folktales follow this arc. Stories about people who gain something are both compelling and memorable. There are as many methods for learning and remembering stories as there are people. Many people remember best by talking. The more frequently they tell a certain story, the more naturally it evolves into a shareable tale. Other people remember best if they can see the images of the story. Drawing the story out into a storyboard, like a cartoon, really helps firm up the details of the story in these people's minds. Still, others need to write the story out word for word, exactly the way they want to tell the story; then they will read that version whenever they are asked to share it.

There is no one proper way to remember a story. The bottom line is this: the more you share it, the more you remember it, and the more others remember it. Since key identity stories are so important for families, never assume once is enough! Don't panic. We know this can be scary, but there are some core actions that will make it easier.

# Action Steps

### Step 1: Declare Your Intent

Be purposeful. Pick a day and time (over a good dinner or when we kneel down for family prayer works best for us). We are not suggesting you announce that you expect everyone to come to dinner with a great story. Such an announcement will actually terrify people and shut them down. The key to family story sharing is letting it evolve in a natural way. It starts with one. It starts with you.

We recognize that this may be a shift in your family dynamic. There may be a need for you to model the behavior for a while. Our conversation around the campfire with Stuart got a little help from a deck of cards filled with memory-prompting questions. You can find many such tools in bookstores and online. But such tools only work if you are willing to lead the discussion and use them. What really matters is that you are prepared to lead out with questions.

Don't bombard your family; just causally introduce a question and see where it leads. We are pretty sure we covered fifty questions during our campfire with Stuart. The next year, when we invited the entire family to join us, we simply asked, "What are you thankful for?" Everyone in the family took a turn and from then on the conversation flowed.

## Step 2: Turn Off Distractions
We know this sounds horrifying, but it is vitally important in order for story sharing to begin. People may think they can update Facebook and participate in a quality face-to-face conversation at the same time, but it simply isn't true. Family storytelling needs to be free flowing, bouncing back and forth between one another. It is sometimes fast-paced and rarely endures interruption or distraction well.

## Step 3: Take Notes
You may think you will remember everything you hear while stories are being told, but it's not likely. The more you write down, or record, the clearer the memory will be for you when you share it later. These can be bullet points just for your use. Don't stop somebody telling a story and ask them to repeat themselves. Visible note taking can kill the moment if you aren't careful. This is a process. You are reintroducing your family to the art form of storytelling. Let it flow freely, but know where you want to steer the conversation next.

## Step 4: Involve Multiple Generations
We have found that involving more generations in the storytelling process increases your likelihood of hearing good stories. Of course, the same incident may be remembered in vitally different ways, but that's okay. Discovering how differently each family member remembers the same story is half the fun anyway. We have seen aged sisters debate over who is the oldest and brothers and sisters tell the same incident as if the other wasn't there. It's great fun to bring in all those varied perspectives!

## Step 5: Be Creative in Ways of Stimulating Memory

Don't just stick to the sweet stuff. Some of the best conversations revolve around favorite holidays, crazy vacations, or parties. Also, times when someone felt afraid, family members got into trouble, or your most awkward and funny moments make for good conversation, too. Use the key identity stories we identified as themes and create questions to harvest those tales.

You may need to create field trip-type experiences to trigger the memories. Take the whole family to a thrift store or an antique store. Gather around the family photo albums or digital photo files. Watch old family movies and record the witty narration of your audience. Also, every home has a junk drawer or two. Invite your family to rifle through it and talk about the memories it triggers. Look around your house. What is on your shelves and walls? Why are those things there? Are there stories behind them? Do the kids have memories of their own regarding the décor? Believe us, simply starting out with "remember the time . . . " can fill your evenings with family memories and stories.

## Step 6: Set Some Ground Rules

Now that your family culture includes telling stories, you need to recognize that everyone tells stories differently. Some family members will talk for hours and dominate the conversation while others won't be able to get more than a few words out at a time. Others will try to talk over everyone else and correct the other person's version of the story. Obviously, these conflicting styles can breed conflict and contention if you are not careful. So make it a rule that no one can correct the story of another while it is being told. There can be no interruptions. It's not about who is right; it's about what they remember. Thus, every shared memory is correct for the person sharing the memory! Encourage everyone to tell their story in ten sentences or less. The chatty ones will be reined in and the quiet ones will have a goal to shoot for.

## Step 7: Create Opportunities for Continued Sharing of Story

No one can resist a good story, especially one in which the teller is the star. Telling your family's stories frequently not only insures they will be remembered; it builds and strengthens family unity. Read on for some fun ways to keep the stories flowing.

# Family Story Slam

**Tools:**

- A few sets of judges who will score stories on a scale of 1–10
- A scorekeeper and scoreboard
- A timekeeper with a kazoo or noisemaker
- Family storytellers
- A fabulous prize
- A theme such as "Remember the time?" "I've never been so afraid!" "Wasn't that funny?" "I knew I was in trouble when . . . "
- Family

**Process:** *The Moth* of New York City (www.themoth.org) created the concept of a story slam. It's hip, urban, and it is usually not the place for families, but the idea is golden. Their model inspired the *Family Story Slam* concept. Sometimes family stories can get a little tired or worn out. Or the details begin to fade because we have condensed them into family shorthand. This game is a great way to freshen up the stories and fan the flames of good-natured family competition in the process.

Put the names of everyone who wants to share a story in a hat. The timekeeper will draw their names one at a time. They will then have only five minutes to tell their tale. If they go over, the timekeeper makes some noise. Now they have twenty seconds to wrap it up. If they fail, the timekeeper lovingly silences them.

Next, the judges score the story. There are only three criteria: Was it on time? Was it a story? Was it on topic? They rate the criteria on a scale of 1–10 and call out their scores to the scorekeeper, who keeps tally on a board everyone can see. The winner gets a prize!

**Rules:**

- Story must be true and from your life
- Story must be told in five minutes or less
- Story must be told live, without notes
- Story may be told by one or more people together, but must not exceed five minutes

**Extra Tips:**

- Clarify your memories
- Plan your story beforehand and remember it's not a story unless it leads listeners through an incident ending in some sort of improvement, discovery, or learning experience
- Practice so you can keep it down to five minutes

# Gratitude Ball

**Tools:**
- One large, inflatable, white beach ball
- Multiple permanent markers
- Family

**Process:** This is best done during a reunion or family gathering. Invite family members to participate in this activity throughout your time together. Instruct them to draw or write things they are grateful for on the ball. People of all ages can do this. It's not about artistic ability; it's about expressing gratitude in ways that make sense for the individual. You will be amazed by how seriously the little ones take this and by what they come up with!

At the close of your time together, everyone shows what they drew and talks about what those pictures mean to them. It's a great way to keep folks busy, get them laughing, and get them talking without them feeling like they are on the spot. Plus, the ball holds memories long after the gathering is over. Every time you get back together, the ball is available for play and remembering. Fun, fun!

**Rules:**
- Designate sections of the ball for each family member
- Family members may only draw in their designated area
- Adults may help younger children, but only if requested by the younger child

# Storytime—Family Style

**Tools:**

- Recording devices, whether audio or just a pencil and paper
- Willing interview subjects
- Family

**Process:** Let youth in your family interview the older members. Kids love this. Let them create the questions they want to ask. You will love what they come up with. Here is just a small list of questions we have witnessed grade school children create:

- *What changes in technology have you witnessed in your life?*
- *Tell me about a time you faced a bad guy.*
- *Was there ever a time you've forgotten an important event?*
- *Did you ever go on a date or to a party that you didn't want to, but it turned out better than you expected?*
- *What kinds of trouble did you get into?*
- *What would you do if you were left home alone when you were a kid?*
- *Tell me about the first time you ever used a computer.*

Obviously, children have things they want to know about! Giving them the opportunity to ask their questions opens everyone up to all sorts of memories, and the children will discover that with every answer comes the inspiration for another question. Once the interviews are complete, kids can choose what stories they want to share at the next family gathering. Make a big deal of this. Let the subjects of the interview be the special guests as the youth tell their stories. This one never gets old either, and every time a story is told, another memory will be discovered.

**Rules:**

- Only children can come up with interview questions
- Adults must answer children's questions, bar none

# Your Story in 150 Words or Less

**Tools:**

- Time to think
- Pencil and paper or a word processing program
- Family

**Process:** One more tip for family story fun. In 2012, the *Reader's Digest* issued a challenge to their readers to tell a true-life story in 150 words or less. The results were outstanding and can be found in the March 2012 issue. When we are challenged to simmer down our experiences to the essential elements of the story, they can become extremely memorable.

Try this exercise as a family. Choose a theme and challenge everyone in the family to create a story from their life that matches the theme, but it must be told in 150 words or less. Print out all the stories and take turns reading them aloud. This can be done over and over again based on whatever theme you choose to focus on. An especially fun theme is "You may not have known this, but . . . "

**Rules:**

- Don't exceed 150 words

# Family Book Club

**Tools:**

- A copy of your chosen book for each member of the family
- A list of discussion topics from the book
- A scheduled date to discuss the book together
- Family

**Process:** The stories of others are great resources. We certainly all enjoy reading such stories, but the reading and discussion of other's tales spawns a whirlwind of our own stories and memories. Choose a book that everyone in the family is interested in reading. Older children and parents can help younger children read the story. Perhaps you can plan time to read the story together or all read the book on your own.

Either way, develop a list of questions for discussion upon completion of the reading. The folks in your family will care more about the questions if you develop them together. Be sure some of these questions prompt family story telling (e.g., what story from your own life does this story remind you of?).

**Rules:**

- Pick a book together that everyone will enjoy reading
- Develop a list of questions together before beginning your book
- Don't make this activity a chore by following up on progress
- Carry on with the discussion on your planned date even if everyone isn't finished

# Burning Hardships

**Tools:**

- Pens and slips of paper
- The story of a hardship you have faced or are currently facing
- A hat
- A fire
- Family

**Process:** Gather around the fire with your family. Begin by sharing the story of a hardship you have faced or are currently facing. We know it is hard to share such stories, but others are much more likely to open up if you do it first! Try to share a story your family hasn't heard before.

Hand out several slips of paper and a pen to each family member and invite them to write key words reminding them of hardships in their lives. Put the slips of paper in a hat. Randomly draw out a hardship and invite the family to discuss the details of this trial. Burn the piece of paper. As it burns, discuss how it feels to watch it burn and reflect on lessons learned from facing that particular trial. Repeat until the slips are gone or the family is no longer engaged in the activity.

**Rules:**

- You need to be the first one to share a story
- Don't force discussion over trials if family members aren't ready to discuss it
- Ensure everyone has an opportunity to share
- Don't force individuals to share if they would rather not participate

# Family Adventures

**Tools:**

- A calendar
- A budget
- Family

**Process:** Sit down as a family and plan out your next adventure together. Know in advance how much money you can spend and make this clear from the beginning. Plan an activity and a date and then carry it out. Ideas for family adventures could include walking to a nearby park, going to your local zoo, attending a local festival, or going on a family vacation.

**Rules:**

- This is a family plan, so ensure all family members have an opportunity to help
- Carry out your plan (no excuses!)

# Warm Fuzzies

**Tools:**
- A shoebox
- Decorating supplies (paper, markers, scissors, stickers, glue, etc.)
- Small slips of paper and pen
- A story of a time when a compliment meant a great deal to you
- Family

**Process:** Tell your family a story about a time when a compliment meant a great deal to you and made a big difference in your life. These stories are sometimes buried, but they are easy enough to find. Think about the people you love most. Why do you love them? Why do they love you? Discuss the impact kindness can have on a person and declare your intention to bring more kindness into family life.

Decorate your family "warm fuzzy" mailbox together. We all remember making such mailboxes for Valentine's Day in elementary school. Allow your family to decorate the box however they would like to. Keep a stack of papers and a pen next to your mailbox and encourage family members to write kind things about other family members throughout the weeks. Choose a day each week or month to review these warm fuzzies as a family.

**Rules:**
- No micromanaging the look of your family's mailbox; make this a family affair
- Review warm fuzzies before the scheduled day of sharing to ensure all family members will receive compliments
- Write compliments for those family members who are not yet included

# Toilet Tales

**Tools:**
- Spiral notebook
- Ballpoint pen
- Toilet in the bathroom the family uses most
- Family

**Process:** At the start of each week, create a question you want your family to answer and write it in the notebook. You may be the only one who answers for a week or two, but once others join in, this party will have a life of its own. Tie a pen to your family memory notebook and place it on top of the toilet tank lid. Once a month, gather the family together and share the contents. Keep track of suggested questions for the future.

**Rules:**
- No editing the work of others
- No removing the notebook from the bathroom

# Family Sharing Board

**Tools:**

- A whiteboard or chalkboard with writing tools
- Sample questions
- Family

**Process:** Post the whiteboard or chalkboard in a prominent place in your home. Discuss as a family specific questions you would like to write on your board. Questions that can be answered with a relatively small number of words work best for this activity. What are you most grateful for? What miracles have you witnessed? What do you like most about yourself?

Leave a question up for a designated amount of time, say a week or a month, and allow family members to answer the question at will during that period of time. This activity will encourage story sharing around the dinner table and throughout the week. After the designated amount of time has passed, erase the question and write a new question.

**Rules:**

- Allow all family members to help develop the questions
- Don't require everyone to answer; some questions will be easier for certain individuals as opposed to others
- Stick to your designated timeline and change the question on a regular basis

# Thomas Edison Night

**Tools:**

- Prepare a story about Thomas Edison
- Prepare a story about a failure in your life that turned into a success
- A light bulb and permanent marker for each member of the family
- Family

**Process:** Begin by telling the story of Thomas Edison's failures. An Internet search will bring this story up quickly. Did you know Thomas Edison failed over one thousand times before he succeeded at creating the light bulb? And now look at what his one success amidst so many failures has done for the world!

Share a story of a failure in your life that has become a success. Invite family members to think of their own failures and share these with the family. If they don't see how their failure is a success, encourage family members to share successes they have seen from the failures of others.

Give each family member a light bulb and marker and ask them to write their successes on the light bulb. Exchange this new "success" bulb for light bulbs in lamps throughout the house so each light turned on is a palpable reminder of family success stories. Share these stories with people who come into your home and see your success bulbs.

**Rules:**

- No story of failure can be left unresolved; be prepared to creatively help family members see success in their stories
- No downplaying the failures of others even if they seem silly; remember that values differ by the individual, and so you should respect the difficulty of others

# Family History Hunts

**Tools:**

- Internet access
- Ancestors' full names
- Ancestors' birth and death dates

**Process:** Gather your family around the screen and do Internet searches for your ancestors. Enter the full names of ancestors in the search bar, along with the year of each ancestor's birth and death. You may be surprised what comes up. There are all sorts of groups collecting data your family may not be aware of. We have downloaded thousands of pages of family history via this process. Each unknown record leads to a bevy of new stories. Plan to share the stories you find at a planned future event.

**Rules:**

- Don't do this alone
- Stick to the subject of your ancestor
- Record the website and date accessed whenever you download information

# Folktales, History, Myth, and Legend

**Tools:**

- Your public library
- Internet access
- Your family library
- Storytelling festivals

**Process:** When we are talking about family stories, it is easy to assume they all have to be personal and true. However, there is great wisdom found in folktales and the historical tales of others. The more stories we know, the more likely we are to find what we need when we need it.

Teresa once wrote a story combining United States Civil War history with a classic motif from a folktale. In the story, the wife must tame a mountain lion before she can receive a black magic potion to make her husband act like he did before the war. She tames the mountain lion but learns in the process that she doesn't need black magic; she just needs to give her husband the same respect, patience, and nurturing she gave the mountain lion.

Teresa told that story for years before Stuart got sick. Then one night she went out to tell it again. It had been a tough day, and she was frustrated with her husband's pain-induced mood swings and limitations. She just wanted to tell the story and move on. But somewhere in the middle of the storytelling, her heart reminded her stories have a purpose. While she had created this story for others, wasn't it possible she had also created it for herself? With the thought came a shift in how she viewed the story.

Suddenly the wife and husband were she and Stuart. The actions of the wife became her own, and she and her husband were the ones who benefitted. Lesson learned, she went home with a new perspective and literally walked her talk based on the story she had told herself. It made a dramatic difference not in how her husband responded but in how she felt about the situation. The message of this fictional story contained powerful truths Teresa desperately needed to hear. Knowing the story improved her reality.

So where can a family find such stories? Start in the folktale section of your local library. That's 398.2 in the Dewey decimal system. These books may contain small print and few pictures, but the stories are classics. They have been told for generations across all sorts of socioeconomic and cultural backgrounds and have withstood the test of time. They contain profound lessons wrapped cleverly in story. Some cultures actually use the telling of such tales to inform behavior. Rather than receiving a lecture and reprimand, the disobedient child is invited to listen to a story. No lectures of morals are attached—just the pure telling of the story. Eventually, the lessons sink in. The stories also become a reference point for the future. It is easier to discuss the misdeeds of a fictional character than it is to discuss our own.

You can also visit the children's section of the library. Children's literature is filled with incredible illustrations these days. What is lacking in words is made up for in stunning visual imagery. Teresa has found there are no age limits when it comes to enjoying a good story. Whenever she begins to read a children's book out loud, everyone in the room (adults and children alike) stops what they are doing and listens, craning their necks to see the pictures. Stories and their lessons linger in the minds of the listeners long after books are closed. While you are at the library, be sure to look for storyteller CDs; they are another fantastic source for being introduced to new stories.

Another wonderful place to introduce your family to the varied delights of story is at a storytelling festival. We are blessed to live in an age when storytelling festivals are dotting the world. If you can find one nearby, it is worth the time and effort to get there. Our family has been attending storytelling festivals for over twenty years. From them we not only created marvelous shared experiences but also gained an arsenal of story to remember and tell each other time and again. In times of family turmoil, it is not uncommon to hear one of us say, "This reminds me of a story we heard at the festival . . . " A great source for finding storytelling festivals is through the National Storytelling Network calendar: http://www.storynet.org/events/calendar.php.

Finally, return to the stories you loved as a child. What resonated with you then may very well be what you need now. Teresa was obsessed with *Nancy Drew* books when she was a preteen. She loved problem solving and mystery. When Stuart got sick, she discovered looking at the situation like Nancy Drew became very helpful. She literally became a detective in regard to Stuart's health care. Often the stories we were drawn to as children contain the lessons we need as adults.

**Rules:**

- Look at the world with story seeking eyes
- Share the stories you find over and over again

# Resources

Allsburg, Chris Van. *The Polar Express*. New York: Houghton Mifflin Company, 1985.

Atwood, Joan D., and Concetta Gallo. *Family Therapy and Chronic Illness*. New Brunswick, NJ: Aldine Transaction, 2010.

Banks, Ann. "Stop Me If You've Heard This One," *The Daily Beast*, February 6, 2009, http://www.thedailybeast.com/newsweek/2009/02/06/stop-me-if-you-ve-heard-this-one.html.

Bocarro, J., and Janet Sable. "Finding the Right P.A.T.H.: Exploring Familial Relationships and the Role of a Community TR Program in the Initial Years After a Spinal Cord Injury." *Therapeutic Recreation Journal* 37, no. 1 (2003): 58–72.

Boyd, Tommy Vannoy. "Relationship Systems: Exploring the Role of the Emotional System in Understanding Dual Chronic Pain Couples." *Dissertation Abstracts International, Section A: Humanities and Social Sciences* 61, no. 7 (2001): 2935–3249.

Carroll, J. S., W.D. Robinson, E.S. Marshall, L.C. Callister, S.F. Olsen, T.T. Dyches, and B. Mandleco. "The Family Crucibles of Illness, Disability, Death, and Other Losses." In *Strengthening Our Families: An In-Depth Look at the Proclamation on the Family*, edited by David C. Dollahite, 278–92. Salt Lake City, UT: Bookcraft, 2000.

Centers for Disease Control and Prevention. "Chronic Fatigue Syndrome." Last modified May 16, 2012. http://www.cdc.gov/cfs/.

———. "Fibromyalgia." Last modified November 7, 2012. http://www.cdc.gov/arthritis/basics/fibromyalgia.htm.

———. "FAQs about Hepatitis B Vaccine (Hep B) and Multiple Sclerosis." Last modified February 8, 2011. http://www.cdc.gov/vaccinesafety/Vaccines/multiplesclerosis_and_hep_b.html.

Clark, Taralyn. "A Qualitative Exploration of Family Strength and Unity in Family Crucibles." Master's thesis, Brigham Young University, 2012.

Cohen, Richard M. *Blindsided: A Reluctant Memoir.* New York: HarperCollins, 2005.

Crandal, Mary Branagan. "Autobiography of a Noble Woman." *The Young Woman's Journal* 6 (1895): 266–67.

Donoghue, Paul J., and Mary E. Siegel. *Sick and Tired of Feeling Sick and Tired: Living with Invisible Chronic Illness.* New York: W. W. Norton, 2000.

Dupuis, Sherry L., and Bryan J. A. Smale. "Bittersweet Journeys: Meanings of Leisure in the Institution-Based Caregiving Context." *Journal of Leisure Research* 32, no. 3 (2000): 303–40.

Eaton, Rob. "Divinely Directed Diversions." BYU–Idaho. Last modified January 19, 2010. http://www2.byui.edu/Presentations/Transcripts/Devotionals/2010_01_19_Eaton.htm.

Estess, Jenifer. *Tales from the Bed: A Memoir.* New York: Atria Books, 2004.

Folkman, Susan, and Judith Tedlie Moskowitz. "Positive Affect and the Other Side of Coping." *The American Psychologist* 55, no. 6 (2000): 647–54.

Glaser, Barney Galland, and Anselm Leonard Strauss. *Awareness of Dying.* Hawthorne, NY: Aldine, 1965.

Grealy, Lucy. *Autobiography of a Face.* New York, NY: Houghton Mifflin, 1994.

Habeeb, Lee, and Leven, Mike. "After the Crack-Up." *National Review* online. Last modified November 28, 2012. http://www.nationalreview.com/articles/334080/after-crack-lee-habeeb?pg=1&goback=%2Egde_1026967_member_191110196#.

Kearney, Geraldine. "Strength in Unity[ES1]." *Australian Nursing Journal* 16, no. 9 (2009): 48.

Keitner, Gabor I., Richard Archambault, Christine E. Ryan, and Ivan W. Miller. "Family Therapy and Chronic Depression." *Journal of Clinical Psychology* 59, no. 8 (2003): 873–84.

Leone, Marianne. *Knowing Jesse: A Mother's Story of Grief, Grace, and Everyday Bliss.* New York, NY: Simon & Schuster, 2010.

Lorig, Kate, Halsted Holman, David Sobel, Diana Laurent, Virginia González, and Marian Minor. *Living a Healthy Life with Chronic Conditions.* Boulder, CO: Bull, 2006.

Mayo Clinic staff. "Multiple Sclerosis: Symptoms." Mayo Clinic. Last modified December 15, 2012. http://www.mayo clinic.com/health/multiple-sclerosis/DS00188/DSECTION=symptoms.

McDaniel, Susan H., Jeri Hepworth, and William J. Doherty. *Medical Family Therapy: A Biopsychosocial Approach to Families with Health Problems.* New York, NY: Basic Books, 1992.

———, eds. *The Shared Experience of Illness: Stories of Patients, Families, and Their Therapists.* New York, NY: Basic Books, 1997.

"Melioidosis." Wikipedia. Last modified April 15, 2013. http://en.wikipedia. org/wiki/Melioidosis.

*New Oxford American Dictionary.* 2nd ed. Oxford, UK: Oxford University Press, 2005.

Pritchard, Joseph. "The Long Term Effects of General Anesthesia." Livestrong. Last modified March 19, 2011. http://www.livestrong.com/article/255374-the-long-term-effects-of-general-anesthesia/.

Radina, M. Elise. "Breast Cancer-Related Lymphedema: Implications for Family Leisure Participation." *Family Relations* 58, no. 4 (2009): 445–59.

Radina, M. E., and Jane M. Armer. "Post-Breast Cancer Lymphedema and the Family: A Qualitative Investigation of Families Coping with Chronic Illness." *Journal of Family Nursing* 7, no. 3 (2001): 281–99.

Robinson, W. David, Jason S. Carroll, and Wendy L. Watson. "Shared Experience Building Around the Family Crucible of Cancer." *Families, Systems & Health* 23, no. 2 (2005): 131–47.

Rogers, Nancy Brattain. "Family Obligation, Caregiving, and Loss of Leisure: The Experiences of Three Caregivers." *Activities, Adaptation & Aging* 24, no. 2 (1999): 35–49.

Rolland, John S. *Families, Illness, and Disability.* New York, NY: Basic Books, 1994.

Scholastic. "Klutz History." Klutz. Accessed January 7, 2013. www.klutz.com/ index/page/static/subpage/history.

Scholl, K. G., L.H. McAvoy, J.E. Rynders, and J.G. Smith. "The Influence of an Inclusive Outdoor Recreation Experience on Families That Have a Child with a Disability." *Therapeutic Recreation Journal* 37, no. 1 (2003): 38–57.

Shellenbarger, S. "Life Stories: Children Find Meaning in Old Family Tales." *Wall Street Journal* online. Last modified March 11, 2009. http://online.wsj. com/article/SB123673699703791017.html.

Stinnett, Nick, and John DeFrain. *Secrets of Strong Families*. Boston, MA: Little, Brown, and Company, 1985.

Whittlesey, Lee H. *Death in Yellowstone: Accidents and Foolhardiness in the First National Park*. Lanham, MD: Roberts Rinehart Publishers, 1995.

# About the Authors

Taralyn is the office manager at Brigham Young University's Aspen Grove Family Camp and Conference Center. She received her associate and bachelor degrees from BYU–Idaho in international studies and sociology, respectively. She also completed her master's degree at BYU in youth and family recreation.

Taralyn has spent most of her professional life working with at-risk children, teens, and families in various therapeutic and recreational settings, helping them adapt to significant life changes including those caused by drug and alcohol addiction, sexual addiction, orphanage, chronic illness, divorce, the challenges of children with special needs, and the death of close friends and family members. She is a teacher, researcher, published author, blogger, and website editor, and she has served as an administrator in camp and rehabilitative settings.

She was reared in a home where story was used to help the family adapt to new and trying situations in family life. Her father's ongoing battle with chronic illness grants her an insider's perspective of what life's crucibles can do to families. She has dedicated her life to strengthening homes and families by helping others to create powerful healing memories and remember the power of their own stories.

Teresa has a liberal arts degree from BYU–Idaho with an emphasis in history, writing, and sewing. She also has a special track in LDS seminaries and institute training. Her twelve years of intensive teaching artist training (received through the Idaho Commission on the Arts) and decades of participation in storytelling workshops with master artists create the foundation of her professional work. Teresa is a national award-winning storyteller and conference presenter who is passionate about using story as a vehicle to turn and heal hearts, and has spent over twenty years practicing her craft with at-risk youth, women, the elderly, and families.

She has received several grants supporting her work with at-risk youth, caregivers for the terminally ill, and storytelling event productions. For years, Teresa has passionately advocated for storytelling on the local, regional, and national level both as producer and administrator. She is a storyteller, teacher, published author, researcher, blogger, and most importantly, a wife, mother, and grandmother. Her ongoing support of a husband with chronic illness grants her a frontline view of the risk-filled, ever-changing world such a situation creates.

The combined experiences Taralyn and Teresa share with at-risk youth and families both in the field and classroom have given them a unique perspective, blending the tools Teresa has gained from twenty years as a professional storyteller with Taralyn's decade of experience working in youth and family recreation. They are a mother/daughter team who has been up close and personal with various chronic illnesses, mental illness, death, drug and alcohol abuse, sexual addiction, divorce, and many other towering mountains families climb on a daily basis.

# About the Publisher

**Familius** was founded in 2012 with the intent to align the founders' love of publishing and family with the digital publishing renaissance which occurred simultaneously with the Great Recession. The founders believe that the traditional family is the basic unit of society, and that a society is only as strong as the families that create it.

Familius' mission is to help families be happy. We invite you to participate with us in strengthening your family by being part of the Familius family. Go to www.familius.com to subscribe and receive information about our books, articles, and videos.

Website: www.familius.com
Facebook: www.facebook.com/paterfamilius
Twitter: @paterfamilius1 and @familiustalk
Pinterest: www.pinterest.com/familius

CPSIA information can be obtained at www.ICGtesting.com
Printed in the USA
BVOW08s0035291013

334893BV00001B/3/P